UNBELIEVABLE BUT TRUE

UNBELIEVABLE BUT TRUE

THE STORY OF MY LIFE

ROBERT WYNGAERT

Copyright © 2021 by Robert Wyngaert

All rights reserved.

No part of this book may be reproduced in any form or by any electronic or mechanical means, including information storage and retrieval systems, without written permission from the author, except for the use of brief quotations in a book review.

To Barbara; my soulmate and the love of my life.
To my children: Linda, Danny, and Sandra.
To my Grandchildren: Chelsea, Amanda, Rikki, Steve, Paul, and Eric.
To my Great-Grandchildren: Harry and Nathan.

JP, Sandra, Paul, Amanda, me, Chelsea, Steve, Rikki, Barbara, Rudy, Linda, and Danny.

CONTENTS

Foreword   xi

Part I
THE EARLY YEARS

Chapter 1	3
Chapter 2	14
Chapter 3	23
Chapter 4	32
Chapter 5	42
Chapter 6	49
Chapter 7	58
Chapter 8	68

Part II
BAR-B-DELIGHT

Chapter 9	93
Chapter 10	112
Chapter 11	116
Chapter 12	121
Chapter 13	129
Chapter 14	133

Part III
CAMPING ALOUETTE

Chapter 15 — 143
Chapter 16 — 152
Chapter 17 — 156
Chapter 18 — 159
Chapter 19 — 166
Chapter 20 — 173
Chapter 21 — 179
Chapter 22 — 182
Chapter 23 — 186
Chapter 24 — 196
Chapter 25 — 203
Chapter 26 — 208
Chapter 27 — 217
Chapter 28 — 227
Chapter 29 — 234
Chapter 30 — 245
Chapter 31 — 251
Chapter 32 — 256

Part IV
RETIREMENT

Chapter 33 — 269
Chapter 34 — 274
Chapter 35 — 280
Chapter 36 — 285
Chapter 37 — 293

Chapter 38	302
Chapter 39	309
Chapter 40	314
Chapter 41	319
Chapter 42	329
Chapter 43	334
Chapter 44	342
Chapter 45	348
Chapter 46	351
Epilogue	364
Wyngaert Wealth Essentials	369
Amanda Lynn Petrin	373
Johanne Wyngaert	375
Acknowledgments	377
About the Author	379

FOREWORD

I decided to write my autobiography on March 11th, 2013, with the assumption that at seventy-five years old, my biggest adventures were behind me. However, even as I wrote about all the lessons I learned during my many years on earth, I kept experiencing new miracles and discoveries.

It would take many books to go through everything that happened after this one leaves off, but it just goes to show that your life story doesn't end until your time comes. And even then, the hope is that you've

FOREWORD

touched enough people, and left enough of a Legacy that your story continues years after you're gone.

I wrote this autobiography to share the principles and values that guided my life. I am eighty-three years old, and not only do they still stand, but I am constantly reminded how important they are.

I was never an expert or a professional in all of my life's creations and accomplishments.

However, I always did the best I could with what I had and where I was at any time in my life. Challenging myself to do things that others wouldn't, or said I couldn't.

With little or no official education, I always had to rely on professionals and books to guide and inspire me. Now, I believe that it is my turn to help others to fulfill their dreams and wishes.

I hope my legacy will inspire others. We

FOREWORD

all have a purpose in life; to make the world a better place. And we only have one lifetime to do it in.

My name is Robert Wyngaert, and this is my unbelievable, yet true story.

I

THE EARLY YEARS

1

"A journey of a thousand miles begins with a single step."
-Chinese Proverb

My parents, Joseph Wyngaert and Suzanne Van Uytfanck, were both born in Belgium, but moved to Canada when they were children, as refugees from World War One. Both of their families arrived with nothing but their suitcases, and were given small farmhouses by the government, which were more like sheds, in Montreal, Quebec. They were very grateful to be accepted in Canada.

Joseph Wyngaert and Suzanne Van Uytfanck on their wedding day.

It was in one such farmhouse on Notre-Dame Street that I was born on March 30th, 1938, across from a large industrial factory that manufactured military equipment. I had three older siblings; Irene (born in 1929), Roger (1932), and Georges (1935).

My mother wanted another girl, and I had a head full of thick, curly hair, so she would put me in dresses. Luckily, this didn't last very long, as Palmyre, the baby of the family, was born in 1942. I had trouble pronouncing Palmyre's name at the time, but my father would sometimes call her 'fille', the French word for 'girl'. I misunderstood him and called her 'Fay', but the name stuck. To this day, that is what everyone except the government calls her.

Palmyre (Fay), Georges, Roger, and me.

My mother's mother lived in the house with us, while my father's parents lived in a farmhouse similar to ours, across the street. One night when I was very little, my grandparents' house caught fire. My grandmother managed to make it out, but my grandfather died trying to climb out of the window. I still have an old picture of the two of them together, but I don't really remember him.

One thing I do remember from those

years, is my parents' vegetable farm. They would go to the Bonsecours market every week with a horse and wagon to sell their produce. We were allowed to eat whatever the customers didn't want, so nothing went to waste. This might be where I got my reputation for eating whatever everyone else wouldn't. I do not like throwing food away. I think I get this from my mother, who never made herself her own plate at meals – she just ate what was left on everyone else's plate after they finished.

You see, back then, we had no money. We didn't have indoor plumbing, except a hand pump for water. I would go with my grandmother and a little four-wheel wagon to pick up the coal that fell from box cars along the railway track, so we could use them for heating. Still, there were many days where we went without, so any liquids left out on the counter in the winter would be frozen solid by morning.

On one of those really cold winter days, my brothers and I were playing by a large creek behind our house when we spotted a wooden board on the ice in the middle of it. Roger didn't think the ice was thick enough for us to get to it, but Georges was confident he could make it, and set off to do just that. He was almost at the board when the ice cracked beneath him, and he fell through.

I froze, looking on in horror as Roger sprang into action, quickly and carefully making his way to the hole Georges had disappeared into. I loved both of my brothers, but Roger was six years older and had his own friends, while Georges, who was only three years older, was my best friend. We did everything together.

Roger brought the wooden board over to the edge of the opening, so he could distribute his weight across it more evenly and put his arms into the freezing water to fish our brother out. Later, Georges would tell me he could see the branches under the ice, but couldn't hold onto any of them. Luckily, Roger was able to grab Georges' hat. It was the kind you tied around your neck, so Roger pulled on the hat, and Georges came with it. We rushed him inside and warmed him up, but I will never forget how terrified I was at the thought of losing Georges, or how much I looked up to Roger for saving his life.

OUR LITTLE FARMHOUSE was getting to be very cramped with my parents, five children, and both of my grandmothers, so we moved to Mackayville – now known as Longueuil – on the South Shore of Montreal. My parents enrolled me in the local public school, St-Jean-Eudes, which was run by nuns. It consisted of approximately twelve classrooms; eight for

French students and four for English students. Although we spoke French at home, with the occasional Flemish swear words, my parents put me in the English classroom, so I would have better employment opportunities later on.

It was a smart decision in the long run, but at the time, it made my life very difficult. I did not speak English, I was a foreigner, and I was small and weak; the perfect target for bullies. I would take a longer road home from school to avoid the French kids who wanted to beat me up. My brothers both had their own classrooms, and were therefore unable to protect me. It was a very scary part of my childhood, that might be responsible for my later interest in martial arts, to ensure no one could ever make me feel that way again.

UNBELIEVABLE BUT TRUE

At least once a year, my father would take us boys fishing in the Laurentians. He insisted that we leave the fishing cabin at five in the morning, so we could get to his 'secret' fishing spots without being followed. I would have said he was being paranoid, but we always came home with more fish than any of the other fishermen. We would often take friends with us, and meet up with cousins when we got there.

I hated waking up that early, so one year

I tried to sleep in by pretending I couldn't hear my dad. I thought I was clever, but my dad sent my cousin Pierre – who was six-foot-two and two-hundred pounds – to sit on me until I got up. I never made that mistake again.

AFTER ABOUT THREE years at St-Jean-Eudes, the school board transferred the English students to an old abandoned house on Holmes street, to make more room for French students. This suited me fine, as the new school was much closer to our house. I was fluent in English by then, and I knew how to look after myself. I was still small, but I was wiry and fearless, which quickly garnered me a reputation as someone you did not want to mess with. As you can imagine, this got me into a lot of trouble.

In the middle of my fifth year of elementary school, at twelve years old, I was expelled for fighting – although I would call it defending myself. My parents told me I had two choices: I could find another school, or I could go to work.

I chose the latter.

2

"I am not a product of my circumstances. I am a product of my decisions."
-Stephen Covey

My first paying job was delivering '*Le Courrier du Sud*', the local newspaper, and other advertising materials. My route began on Grande Allée Street, not far from our house, but it covered the main towns of the South Shore: Ville Jacques

Cartier, St-Lambert, Mackayville, and Greenfield Park. Thankfully, it was only three days a week.

My father felt this meant my remaining four days could be spent working for him. He had recently decided it was time to upgrade the family to a more modern house, so he bought land on Grande Allée to build a duplex. This kept me very busy.

Before my father would leave to work as a foreman of maintenance at Canada Packers, he would give me a list of things to do, expecting them to all be done by the time he got home. I had no idea how to frame a wall or install Gyproc, but boy did I learn fast! If something wasn't done properly, or to his satisfaction, I would have to take it down and do it all over again the next day. I hated it at the time, but I learnt some valuable skills that I still use, seventy years later. I have taken on countless major renovations and construction projects throughout my life, seeing them through from conception to completion, stemming from those days with my father.

About a month after my family moved into the duplex I helped build, our old house caught fire due to faulty electrical wiring. We all rushed over and tried to put it out, but the house was made of wood, and we hardly had any water, so all we could do was watch it burn. Thank God no one was inside!

A demolition at my father's work gave him access to some free lumber, so we rebuilt the old house after the fire. Though I was available to him, and knew a lot more about construction this time around, it was still no easy task. Between my job and the construction, I would spend my days off digging holes four feet deep for concrete pillars to support the house, then wake up at 6 a.m. the next day to deliver newspapers. I was spread very thin.

My favorite part was the time I spent with my father's mother, who I fondly called Mémère. Since we were only using secondhand wood for the house, she taught me how to salvage the large wooden planks that were caked with dirt, as well as the long nails inside them. I had to clean each board and pull out all of the nails, then straighten them and segregate by size. It was physically exhausting, but my Mémère was a strong old lady who made it look easy.

My Grandparents.

In April 1952, after building two houses and delivering countless newspapers in extreme weather conditions, I was ready for something less physically challenging. Georges was working for a customs broker on St. James Street in Montreal, so I asked him if he had any ideas. It just so happened that there was an opening as an Office Clerk for another custom broker on McGill Street.

I was fourteen and had just gotten a permit to work, so I went to Daniel Kiely Inc., and met with the owner, Mr. Jack Boyne. I could barely see over the counter where Mr. Boyne, a powerful and physically imposing man, stood.

I wasn't qualified for office work, with my education lacking and all of my experience stemming from construction projects. However, they must have been pretty desperate, because I was hired on the spot. They offered me 18$ a week, which was less than I was making delivering newspapers, but in a much better environment, with great potential for advancement. I accepted without hesitation.

Since we lived on the South Shore and my new job was in Montreal, I travelled back and forth on the Montreal Southern County Railroad. It was about an hour commute, that I usually spent catching up with friends. In the winter, they would have a pot-bellied coal burner stove in the carriages to keep us warm.

Everything about my new job was difficult for me. As a Custom Long Room Man, my responsibilities were delivering and picking up documents from various customers (like a human fax machine), typing up and then mailing documents, as well as processing parcels and packages through customs. I had never considered school to be that important, until I found myself having to read, write and type day in and day out at the office. At the time, there were ads everywhere to get your high school equivalency through correspondence, so I signed up with the American School and completed their courses over the next three years.

I always tried to time my document deliveries so that I was on the road around lunchtime. I didn't always have enough money to make myself a lunch, or to buy one, so I relied on family members. If I was near Woolworths, I could count on my sister Irene, or Denise Laurendeau, the lovely young lady Irene had set Georges up with, to buy me lunch and a slice of apple pie whenever I stopped in. If I was around Bleury Street, my godmother Yvonne would make sure I was well-fed. She was soft and gentle, like my mother, and always made me feel at home.

My family was living comfortably in the second house my father and I built, renting out the duplex, so on my days off, I was able to relax and hang out with my brother, Roger, who had a horse, a goat and a few other animals. He didn't always have money to feed these animals, so he would bring Georges and I to pick up hay along Taschereau Boulevard. It wasn't really hay, but the city maintenance crews would cut all the tall grass and leave it on the side of the road. Once we had a full load, Georges and I would sit on the pile of hay to hold it down, picking apples from the trees as Roger drove us home. Little did we know, those apples were on private property, and one day, the owner sent the police after us. Luckily, the cop was a friend of my dad's, so he let me off with a warning, but I never went near that tree again.

3

"If you love someone, set them free. If they come back, they're yours; if they don't they never were."
-Richard Bach

I started playing football for the Chambly County Flyers, a new team conceived by our coach, Rudy Presner. We would have games against the St. Lambert Combines, the Rosemont Bombers, and the St-Hubert Air Force Base, but we very rarely won. The other teams were better, more experienced, and better equipped than our old helmets, shoulder pads and cleats. It would have been nice to win sometimes, but it was still a lot of fun, and we had some very pretty cheerleaders. At fifteen years old, with a steady job, I was able to catch the attention of many girls my age.

In 1953, Jack Boyne held a year-end celebration at the Ritz Carlton Hotel, and all of the employees were invited. I was single at the time, so I thought I might ask one of our cheerleaders. Instead, my immediate supervisor, Melvin Hedge, offered to set me up on a blind date with a terrific young girl he thought I would really like. Her name was Barbara Thompson, and she was his younger cousin – fifteen years old, just like me.

I can't remember what dress she wore,

but I remember it was very nice, and with her hair all done up she looked like a million bucks. She was some beauty – she still is – and I couldn't believe my luck. My fondest memory of the evening was during the meal, when Barbara was trying to cut her steak. At one point, her knife slid, and she sent peas flying right into my boss' lap at this very fancy dinner. It was embarrassing at the time, and I was foolishly worried I would lose my job over it. We managed to have an excellent time anyway, and laugh about the incident to this day.

FROM THERE, Barbara and I hit it off very quickly. She worked at Northern Electric and lived in Rosemount with her parents, two brothers, and five sisters, ranging from four to eighteen years old.

I still lived on the South Shore, so I had

to ride the train and a couple of buses to get to her house. I loved to take her to Habib's for supper on Saturdays, walks on Mount Royal, or town hall dances with her sister, Joan, and her boyfriend, Bob Smith. As Barbara already had a brother named Bobby, and Joan's boyfriend was Bob, Barbara's little sisters called me 'Wyng-hart'. Considering they had trouble with 'Barbara' and called her 'Wawa', I thought it would have been easier for them to start calling the other Bob 'Smith', but I also found it cute that they gave me a nickname.

AFTER FALLING asleep and missing my stop on the train more than a few times, I helped Roger buy a car, so that he could drive me to Barbara's. At the time, he had a license but no car, while I had money and no license. It seemed like the perfect arrangement.

There was a jeweler, Harry Stein, who worked in the office right next to mine, so for Barbara's sixteenth birthday, I got her a compact for her makeup. It became a tradition over the years, for me to go to him whenever I needed to get her a present.

My family was Catholic. Not that we went to church every Sunday, but we did honor the rule that you can't eat meat on Fridays. One week, wanting to impress her, I brought Barbara to a fancy restaurant. It was a Friday night, so I scoured the menu for something without meat and settled on 'filet mignon'. I wasn't sure what kind of fish it was, but it sounded delicious. Imagine my surprise when the waiter showed up with a fancy, expensive…steak. I couldn't send it back, and I didn't want to let Barb know how silly I had been, so I ate what would later become her favorite cut of meat, feeling guilty the whole time. Thankfully it wasn't a mortal sin!

WHILE BARB WOULD GET ready for our dates, I would sit on the balcony and talk to her father, also a Robert. Our conversations were always interesting, and would often run long, so even after Barbara was ready for me, I would stay there talking to him. Barbara did not appreciate me spending so much of our precious time together talking to her father instead of paying attention to her. Eventually, the combination of those talks, the long distance between our houses, and my determination to play football instead of going dancing with her, became too much, and she ended things with me. She started going out with a man named Axel Swenley, who took her to shows and did the things she wanted me to do.

I was devastated, but I tried my best to

move on. I started dating Mary Meany, a cheerleader who didn't mind spending her time watching my football games. I brought her as my date to our Fundraising Dance at the Royal George School, in Greenfield Park. At the end of the meal, when they announced the winner of the Most Valuable Player of the Year Award, I was shocked to hear my name. I truly appreciated the honor, but I didn't feel like I deserved it as much as most of the other players. When I asked, 'Why me?', they told me it was because they could always rely on me; their offensive and defensive guard. "You block them all, no matter the odds."

A FEW MONTHS LATER, I got a call from Joan, to see if I would be interested in going on a date with Barbara. Apparently, Axel wasn't the guy for her, and I was more than happy to take his place. I had to break up with Mary first, but it worked out well, since she ended up marrying my friend, Pat House.

When I turned eighteen, our football team went bar hopping in Montreal. I wasn't used to drinking – only at a few social events – so the alcohol hit me a little hard. After a few bars, we came across a tattoo parlor. Most of the guys were too scared, or maybe weren't drunk enough yet, but Rudy got a tattoo on his arm. He chose 'Betty', the name of the girl he was in love with.

He suggested I get one as well, for Barbara. I don't know if it was because I was so happy I got her back, or because of the many beers I drank that night, but I eventually gave in and got a heart with 'Barbara' in it on my right forearm.

This was a terrible decision, as I got an

infection from the unsanitary equipment at the parlor. My arm swelled up to double its size, and I needed to take antibiotics to get rid of it.

Things didn't work out so well for Rudy either, as Betty ditched him shortly after we got the tattoos. It turned out that choosing Barbara's name was the only part of the tattoo I didn't regret. As my career advanced, I had to wear long-sleeved shirts to hide it, even in the summer. Not to mention that when you get older, tattoos becomes faded and illegible. Overall, I do not recommend them.

4

"Life is a near-death experience."
-George Carlin

In the spring of 1956, Barbara and I were faced with a dilemma. My brother, Georges, was marrying Denise Laurendeau on May 12th. That same day, Barbara's sister, Joan, was marrying Bob Smith. I wasn't going to miss my brother's wedding, and Barb was her sister's maid of honor, so we were in quite the pickle. I was starting to question whether Barb would forgive me if we each went to separate weddings, but religion saved the day. As my family was Catholic, Georges' wedding was in the morning, at 10 a.m., while Joan, who was Protestant, was getting married in the afternoon. As long as nothing unexpected happened, we should be able to make it to both.

It was a very stressful morning for me, but everything ran on time and we made it to both weddings. I considered the day a success, but something shifted in the way people treated Barbara and I. Now that we were both eighteen and going to weddings together, people started asking us when our wedding would be. When Lilianne, who lived in Barb's building, saw us coming home one day, she asked, "So, when's the wedding?"

My plan was to smile and ignore the question, but Barb said, "Ask him."

I knew I wanted to spend the rest of my life with her, but now I could see I had to do something about it. I went to see Mr. Stein, and the next time someone asked about the wedding, I went along with it. It was only years later that I found out how much it annoyed Barb to hear me talking like our engagement was a given, before I'd even asked her.

On June 20th, I woke up feeling funny, but I still made my way to work, figuring it was just something I ate, and that it would pass. As the day went on, the pain in my stomach got worse, and I'm pretty sure I spiked a fever. I tried to soldier on, but when the pain got so bad that I threw up, I requested permission to leave work early.

Seeing the state of me, my supervisor said yes without hesitation.

I set off for Canada Packers, hoping my dad could drive me home. As I was walking there, the pain got so intense that I knew there was no way I would make it. I used the first phone booth I saw to tell my father I was very sick and needed him to pick me up on Mill Street. By the time he got there, I had collapsed on the sidewalk from the pain.

I was vaguely aware of him carrying me to his car so he could drive us to the hospital. Unfortunately, it was voting day, so the roads were jammed, and we got stuck in heavy traffic. My dad took one look at me and knew I needed medical attention as soon as possible, so he used the sidewalk to pass cars and get me to the closest hospital he could find, which happened to be a maternity one on Sherbrooke Street.

My dad left his car in the middle of the sidewalk and carried me in.

It didn't take long for them to diagnose me with Peritonitis, which meant my appendix had burst, slowly spreading bacteria throughout my body. I needed immediate surgery to remove my appendix, and a course of very strong antibiotics to hopefully kill the bacteria. Ideally, you want to get to the hospital before the appendix bursts, because once it does, your chances of survival diminish significantly. My father's fast thinking – and disregard for the rules of the road – and the doctors saved my life that day. It was the first time I almost died, but it would not be the last.

I DON'T REMEMBER how long I was in the hospital, or much of my recovery, but it was a long time. Every day, without fail, Barbara would come and visit me with homemade lemonade. I don't know what I did to deserve someone like her, but I am so grateful for it.

Barbara and I.

In September, Barbara convinced me to talk to her father about getting a job at Northern Electric, where he was a supervisor. By then, I was making more than double what I started out with at Daniel Kiely, with $42 a week, but Barb was making $80 as an engraver, with a monthly piecework bonus.

I had taken an evening course at the Automobile School of Montreal, thinking I might try being a mechanic, but although I did well in the course – passing with 88% – I did not enjoy the work. Luckily, it wasn't wasted, because it gave me the freedom to take care of my own cars, without having to rely on garages and mechanics.

Her dad spoke to Mr. Brooks in the personnel department, and to my surprise, I was hired to work on relays. I received 1.27$ an hour, plus a monthly piecework bonus. Everything was perfect, with Barb and I both making good money. I bought my first car, a 1952 Monarch, for 700$.

My first car.

That Christmas, Barb came to my parents' house to open presents. She liked staying over because we now had hot running water, and I liked having her close, even if we had to stay in separate bedrooms. That night, I asked Barbara to marry me. I had already asked her parents, who were thrilled. I used the ring I bought from Mr. Stein, and although I knew we were meant to be together, my heart still burst with joy when she said yes.

. . .

We immediately got to work planning our wedding. Barb could finally join in, happily, when people like Lilianne asked when the wedding would be.

In the Summer of 1957, we spent two weeks of our vacation time at Barbara's Aunt's cottage in Lac des Plages, just North of Montreal. On our way there, the weather was far from ideal for an inexperienced driver like me. There was a torrential downpour, where I could hardly see anything in front of me. I drove slow, just to be on the safe side, but even that wasn't enough to save us from sliding off the gravel road when we got to a very steep curve. I managed to maneuver the car so it hit a large tree from the back side, instead of head on. Barb and I were both okay, but my new car was scrapped. We took our bags and walked to a nearby hotel so we could call someone to pick us up.

While we were walking to the hotel, Barb's family got worried about us not being there yet, so her father came looking for us. I never imagined that he would slip on the exact same part of road I did, at a much faster speed, so his car ploughed right into mine. At the speed he was going, if my car hadn't been there to cushion his impact into the tree, I am sure he would have died, or at least been seriously injured. As it was, he met up with us at the hotel, and we took a taxi to the cottage together.

5

"You shouldn't marry the person you can see yourself having a good life with. You should marry the person you know you wouldn't have a life without."
-Unknown

Me and Barbara on our wedding day.

I don't remember much from the months leading up to our wedding, on June 7th 1958. I assume there was some kind of planning, maybe a bridal shower, but I don't think I had a bachelor party. Georges was going to be my best man, with Joan as

Barb's maid of honor, and my tux was rented. All I had to do was wait until the day and say, 'I do'.

That was my plan, but my stress-free world was turned upside down when I was laid off from Northern Electric the day before my wedding. It came completely out of the blue, and all I could do was hope that it wouldn't be long until they called me back. And try not to ruin the wedding over it.

Since I'm Catholic and Barb was raised Protestant, we weren't allowed to get married inside the church, so the ceremony took place behind it. Barb even had to take courses and promise the priest that we would raise our children Catholic when the time came.

When I saw her walking towards me in that dress, I completely forgot about my unexpected layoff and our unconventional ceremony. It was the happiest moment of my life.

After the ceremony, we had a selection of chicken salads and cold cuts for our seventy-five guests. We had a few friends and work colleagues, as well as both of our families. Roger came with his wife, Kay, Georges was at the head table with Denise, Irene came with her husband Rolland, and Fay brought Bruce, a friend of mine from football. While I was the second youngest in my family, Barb was the second oldest in hers, so Joan was the only one of her siblings who came with her husband, Bob Smith.

We left for our Honeymoon in a red, 1954 Pontiac Sedan I got for 800$ with the insurance money from our crash. We went to Atlantic City, but stopped on the way in Lake George, and splurged on a meal at Roberto's. It was so fancy that they had men there to open the doors for us when we walked up. Barb was impressed that they had delicious shrimp the size of her hand, while I was amazed that this beautiful woman was now my wife.

In Atlantic City, we stayed at a Bed and Breakfast, and bought a little stove so we could cook our own meals and not have to spend too much money in restaurants. We spent our days walking along the Boardwalk, too broke to actually do anything that cost money.

The entire trip was 125$, which was all the money I had for it. Luckily gas was only 25 cents a gallon at the time, because I don't think I would have had enough to get us home otherwise.

Me and Barbara on our honeymoon in Atlantic City.

Once we were back in Quebec, Barb and I settled into the bottom floor of my parents' duplex, with Georges and Denise as our upstairs neighbors. We couldn't afford to have our own phone line, so we shared theirs. Whenever there was a call for us, they would bang on the pipes to let us know. Money was tight, but family was never far away, especially with our backyard being linked to my parents'. One thing is

ROBERT WYNGAERT

for sure, Georges, Denise, Barbara and I became very close!

6

"Failure will never overtake me if my determination to succeed is strong enough."
-Og Mandino

That summer, the city was putting in water and sewer lines, so I was able to keep busy by helping my neighbors get hooked up. Backhoes were hard to find in those days, and expensive, but with all of my experience digging for my father's buildings, I was able to perform this very physical work. Those skills also allowed me to help my neighbor build his garage. It was nowhere near what I was making at Northern Electric, but every bit helped.

This was around the time I joined the YMCA's judo club with my good friend Kevin Jones, where I became the secretary-treasurer. It was nice to have a more recreational way to keep in shape, and Harold Tokai, our instructor, taught me so much about strength, the responsibilities of power, and discipline.

Finally, in August, my father helped me get a job at Canada Packers, doing freezer work. I had to bring large boxes of pork trimmings in and out of freezers, then place the frozen product into a large machine that would mince it so it could be turned into bologna and sausages.

I stayed there until March of 1959, when they laid me off due to lack of work, just as

Northern Electric recalled me to be a Mechanical and Electrical Relay Technician. I was very grateful to Canada Packers for getting me out of a tough spot, but it was also nice to not have to lug around frozen meat anymore.

A FEW MONTHS LATER, I woke up in the middle of the night to something that sounded like an explosion. Growing up during the war, I had become used to the blackouts, so I figured all of the preparation had been for this, and we were being attacked. I assumed the steam came from a bomb, so I woke the entire building and brought them outside to safety. It was then, once my brain got over the immediate fear, that I realized it was just a defective thermostat that burst the pipes and blew up our hot water tank. Boy did I feel silly!

We took it as a sign to do some

renovations. Barb and I were both making good money at the Northern again, so we could afford it. We also made some new purchases, like a television, a sofa, curtains, drapes, etc. I had just been laid off when we moved in, but we were now able to make our little house a home.

Denise and Georges.

I also splurged on a 1960 Pontiac Parisienne. It was 4700$, the most expensive car I had purchased by far – in cash no less – but it was brand-new. I had quickly developed a taste for good-looking, expensive, luxury cars, an affliction that still plagues me to this day.

I would drive Barb and I home after work, where my mother would have a wonderful, hot meal waiting for us. My mother was the nicest, sweetest woman you could meet, who always went out of her way to do nice things for other people. Barb is very much like that as well, so on the days she wasn't working, she would go over to my mother's and help her with cleaning and other chores.

Once the work was done, weekends were filled with activities, such as visiting friends and family. It seemed like we were always with Georges and Denise, since they lived so close, but my best friends at the time were Pat House, who you may remember married my ex-girlfriend Mary, and Kevin Jones, who married her sister, Alice. Kevin and I were very involved in our judo training, even competing against other Judo schools, where I would sometimes face Bob Smith. It was a time where we were young, happy, and carefree.

I was perhaps a little too carefree and cocky, so my friends encouraged me to join the Knights of Columbus, a Catholic Fraternal Organization. The night I was sworn in was quite an experience that I will never forget. I would tell you all about it, but then I would have to kill you. Well, not really, but I did swear to not tell anyone what happened. What I can say is that through a series of exercises, they showed me that united we are stronger, while divided we fall.

. . .

IN JANUARY OF 1961, I was asked to transfer to Northern Electric's branch in Belleville, Ontario. I enjoyed my job and could see this was a great opportunity, but Barbara's job, as well as both of our families, were in Montreal. I told them it wasn't possible for me to move to Ontario, but they weren't able to keep me on in my current position, so they laid me off. Again.

Luckily, I had learnt my lesson the first time Northern Electric let me go. In April 1960, when my father told me Canada Packers was looking for part-time workers to do maintenance on weekends, I immediately jumped at the opportunity. Even with my full-time job at the Northern. Extra income never hurts, and I knew it meant I would be in a better position if I got laid off again, which just so happened to be the case.

. . .

It took four months before I was hired at United Aircraft of Canada. As luck would have it, that was the same week Northern Electric asked me to come back to work in another department. Although I liked working at the same place as Barbara, and they were offering almost double what I would make at United Aircraft, I refused their offer. The pay bump with United Aircraft was negligible, but I was excited to be able to work closer to home on the South Shore. Plus, United Aircraft had a much bigger potential for advancement, without me needing to move far away.

After my job at Daniel Kiely taught me the importance of an education, I made it a goal to always be learning, saying yes to every opportunity. I successfully completed training on basic IBM machines from the Data Processing Institute, so I was hired at United Aircraft as a foreman clerk until they got an opening in the computer department.

A foreman's clerk was the lowest paying job they had, making even less than the janitors. The computer department remained out of my reach, but thanks to my supervisor, Ken Bloxham, I was quickly promoted to a general foreman's clerk. From there, it took less than nine months for me to become assistant foreman on first shift. Before long, I was head foreman on second shift. It meant working evenings, which was inconvenient, but I was also the one in charge.

7

"Family is not an important thing. It's everything."
-Michael J. Fox

February 13th 1962 became one of the best days of my life when my beautiful daughter, Linda Susan Wyngaert, was born. Her birth changed my entire outlook on life – I suddenly had big responsibilities. I had to make sure she would always be safe and happy, with a roof over her head and food in her belly. She is the spark that lit the flame inside my heart and made me the man I am today.

When Linda was just a few months old, Barb had to go to the hospital for surgery on her gallbladder. She'd been having issues since the beginning of her pregnancy, but the doctors had to wait for Linda to be born before they could do anything about it. Back then, fathers weren't nearly as hands-on as they are now, and we couldn't afford to have me take the time off work to take care of Linda while Barb was gone. So, we brought Linda to stay with Barb's mom, Ina.

Before she went to the hospital, Barb gave her mother a list of rules and things that Linda would need, all based on 'The Common Sense Book of Baby and Child Care' by Doctor Spock. Ina, who had already raised eight children, promptly threw the list in the garbage and trusted her own instincts as soon as Barb was out the door.

Our house on Laurier Street.

In early 1963, Fay's boyfriend, Bruce, was helping his aunt sell her three-bedroom house at 1551 Laurier Street. Barb was pregnant with our second child, so the duplex would soon be cramped, and I really wanted to own my house, rather than paying my dad rent. It was quite the fixer-upper, so I was able to buy it for only 3000$, thus becoming a homeowner. The house wasn't livable, so Barb insisted that I do some major renovations before she would even consider moving in. I managed to make the ground floor acceptable to Barbara just before our son, Daniel Robert Wyngaert, was born on April 4th.

While Linda was my beautiful baby girl, Danny was the son I always wanted, who I could teach things to, and would eventually take after me. Only his name wasn't meant to be Danny.

On the day of our son's baptism, Barbara was still recovering, so she didn't come to the church with us. We had decided we would name him Steven, but once I got inside, with the priest looking down at me, I got nervous and couldn't remember the name anymore. When the priest asked me, I froze, and my mother said, "Daniel," which then became his name. Barb was definitely not happy with me.

IN 1964, Canada Packers was looking for a foreman to watch over their weekend employees. When they discovered that my day job was as a foreman at United Aircraft, they put me in charge of the twenty-two part-time, week-end employees. Our main responsibilities were to clean the plant facilities in depth, which they couldn't do while the plant was in operation. We had to steam wash all of the department floors and equipment, the receiving and shipping docks, the rendering department, the underground tunnel the animals came from, the stockyards across the street, and the smokehouses. Not to mention all the laundry and snow removal. I implemented a system to keep track of how much time each employee spent doing each task, understanding that efficiency was of the essence.

I was able to hire men that I knew to be good workers, like my friend Regis Lemieux, as well as my brother Georges. Roger tried it out for a little while, but he didn't appreciate working under his baby brother's supervision. My dad was already a supervisor, which led some people to think I got the job thanks to him. I quickly proved myself, but my mother asked me to take it easy on Georges, who had a heart condition, so I lightened his load and helped him out when I could. My family connection, as well as how I showed Georges preferential treatment, led to us being called the Brown Brothers. As in brown-nosers.

It was a big blow at first, but as everyone got to see my work ethic and realized that I deserved the position, I stopped seeing it as a taunt and began to own it. My brothers and I from then on referred to ourselves as the Brown Brothers, with pride.

The 'Brown Brothers': Georges, Roger, Fay, me, and my father.

We sometimes got special assignments, such as painting the facility. One day, we were painting the exterior metal fire escape on the tallest building – approximately fifty feet high. None of my men were willing to paint the top portion that led to the roof. I don't believe in asking people to do things I wouldn't be willing to do myself, so I said I would do it.

I am not afraid of heights, but I don't really like them either. As I approached the top, the steel supports broke loose from the roof, leaving me hanging from the ladder in midair. I tried not to panic, hoping the lower supports would hold until I shimmied down. It was clear to everyone there that if the supports gave out, no matter what my men did, I would be a dead man. The silence was deafening, so all I could hear was the rather loud pounding of my own heart, until I finally got to safety. I am not sure what would have happened if someone else had been in my place, but I guess that once more, it just wasn't my time to go.

. . .

IN ADDITION to my full-time job at United Aircraft and my part-time one at Canada Packers, I spent all of my free time renovating our house from top to bottom, interior and exterior. I added a new roof, bricks, changed the windows...I even put in a fence with cartoon character stickers to make the kids smile. Whatever I didn't know how to do, I found people to do it, or to teach me. It was a lot of work.

Barb, in addition to looking after the children, got a job working at the new Dunkin' Donuts with Denise. She stayed there until a few months before January 5th 1965, when Sandra Ann Wyngaert completed our little family. Just as beautiful as her big sister, Sandra filled us both with joy.

Having three kids was a really big responsibility, and I had to make sure I could provide for them. In the sixties, we didn't have things like Medicare and maternity leave, so in the span of three years, we lost half of our family's income, and a huge chunk of my salary went to paying the doctors for three deliveries, and Barb's gallbladder surgery.

Linda, Sandra, me, and Danny.

8

"Believe in yourself. Have faith in your abilities. Without humble but reasonable confidence in your own powers, you cannot be successful or happy."
-Norman Vincent Peale

I was working at Canada Packers on October 9th 1965, while the rest of my family was going to Joan's for her son's birthday party. It wasn't long into my shift that the security guard came and found me, out of breath, like he'd had to look all over for me. All he could tell me was that I had to get to the Notre-Dame Hospital as soon as possible.

I don't know how I managed to drive there, knowing someone I loved was badly injured, or worse, and I didn't even know who. When I got there, they told me that Barb's mother, Ina, had been in a car accident. Barbara's father had been on his way to pick Barb and the kids up with Ina, Bobby, and Ronnie in the car. Luckily, Barb's father and brothers were okay, except for Bobby's concussion, but Ina did not make it.

I still had both of my parents, but my mother-in-law's death devastated me, so I couldn't even imagine what it would do to Barbara. I was the one who had to go home and tell her what happened. I can't remember the words I used, or her reaction in that moment, but it was the hardest thing I've ever had to do in my entire life.

Barbara, as you can imagine, was absolutely destroyed. Everyone was. Ina's death left Mr. Thompson with a house full of young children who had just lost their mother. Joan moved in for a few months to help him out, while Barb and I offered to adopt the two youngest; Marilyne and Donna. Barb's father categorically refused to split up his family, insisting that he would take care of his own children.

THE FOLLOWING YEAR, Joan and Bob Smith were having trouble getting a mortgage for a house. I had a good job and no mortgage of my own, so I made a deal with my brother-in-law. I found a house close to ours, gave the down payment and secured a mortgage, all under my name. I even put in 500$ to renovate it for them. All

Bob had to do was make the monthly payments for me, and once the house was paid off, it would be his. The small catch was that Bob would also have to stay sober. His drinking had definitely hindered their getting a mortgage on their own, and he'd had a tendency to start fights when he was drinking. He'd had a difficult life, attending Shawbridge (a Youth Detention Center) as a boy, but he had recently stopped drinking so he could be the man Joan and his children needed him to be. Instead of dwelling on the mistakes of his youth, Bob used them as a cautionary tale to inspire others to turn their own lives around. He had joined Alcoholics Anonymous to overcome his addiction, then proceeded to sponsor countless others battling their demons. Many of them were strangers who simply needed a hand, but he helped family members too. One of my nieces had a very difficult time when she was younger, and he was instrumental in her recovery. He also introduced one of his sponsees to the person that would become the love of his life for over forty years, helping him to never touch another drop. Bob turned his career around as well, becoming a CN Police Officer to keep people safe.

By early 1973, Bob Smith was still sober, and done paying off the house. Boy did he surprise me by selling it for nearly five times what I paid for it. I co-signed with him for a beautiful new house on Montgomery Street. Bob Smith had completely turned his life around for his family.

Now that Sandra, our youngest, was a year old, Barb went back to work at Northern Electric, and we hired Mrs. Drummond to watch the kids while we were gone. She had already raised three children of her own and was an absolute godsend.

Barb was doing shiftwork, which meant one week she would work days, the next nights, then evenings...it was all over the place. Mrs. Drummond would pick the kids up before Barb left for work, then would bring them back in the evenings to give them their baths, put them to bed, and wait for me to get home from Vic Tanny's, where I exercised after work. Mrs. Drummond loved our children and went above and beyond what a babysitter should do, like crocheting the kids clothes and teaching Barbara how to drive. All of this for 28$ a week, which we considered a bargain.

IN 1967, my supervisor, Ken Bloxham, left United Aircraft. The city was offering grants to build accommodations for visitors to Expo67, so he took them up and built a campground on an airstrip with his friend, Dan Hayes. They made a killing that

Summer, so Ken decided to sell all of the apartment buildings he owned, so he could run the campground in the summer and spend his winters in Florida. Ken was known at work as the Gentle Giant, due to his imposing frame and kind demeanor. When he proposed that I buy one of his apartment buildings for 35000$, I told him he was crazy if he thought I could afford something like that. Not only did he explain to me that the rents would cover the mortgage, he co-signed it for me. Ken was a good guy, and I trusted him, so I went for it and bought his apartment building.

One of my first renters was Barb's sister, Doreen. She was moving to the South Shore from Montreal, and having trouble finding a place big enough for her family of five. I was glad to be able to help them out, but slightly apprehensive about the investment as a whole.

. . .

As it turned out, Ken was right about the rents covering the mortgage, but they didn't cover the repairs that come along, or big-ticket items, like replacing hot water tanks. You also have to be on-call 24/7, in case something ever happens. I got a friend, René-Paul Paquin, to help me take care of any emergencies if I wasn't available. Mostly if it involved plumbing, which was his specialty.

One winter night, I got a call at two o'clock in the morning, saying that water was leaking into the bedroom of one of the upstairs apartments. I called and left a message with Paquin's wife, since water leaks tended to be his domain, and headed to the apartment to shovel the roof. The ladder I had was shorter than I would have liked, so it rested against the building, and I had to hoist myself onto the actual roof. I went around and shovelled off all of the snow, then resigned myself to climb back down the ladder, knowing I would have a considerable drop. I looked around in the dark, but try as I might, I could not find the ladder. As it was resting against the wall instead of sticking up over the roof, I had to stick my head over the ledge to find it. Even then, it was nowhere to be found. Suddenly, the drop from the roof to the ladder was much preferable to the drop from the roof to the ground. At this point, I was either going to have to jump, or freeze to death on the rooftop.

I was contemplating which was better when I heard Paquin shouting my name from below. You cannot imagine the relief I felt at hearing his voice. He found the ladder and guided me to it, then climbed up so he could place my feet on the top rung of the ladder when I hung over the roof's ledge. It was quite the adventure, that I never want to repeat.

. . .

UNBELIEVABLE BUT TRUE

IN 1968, my father offered me a piece of land beside his house on Holmes Street, as a thank you for all of the construction work I had done with him years before. Instead of just building a new house for my family, I decided I would build an apartment building, so we would have somewhere to live, but also earn money from it. I went to the city with plans for what I wanted to build, armed with knowledge from my recently purchased property, but they told me I wasn't able to have windows on one side unless I bought the land beside it. The notary looked up the owner, and I was able to buy the second plot of land for something close to 600$ – where we would one day put in a pool. I didn't have the money to build the apartment, and I had just finished renovating our own house, so I wasn't rolling in credit either. Luckily, my father gave me 15 000$ for my house on Laurier, that I would sell once we moved into the apartment. He charged me 10% interest on the loan, but I wouldn't have been able to do any of it without him. In those days, you couldn't get a mortgage unless the building was already built.

I have had great successes in my life, but none of them would have been possible without the support of my family, and the people who believed in me. Working at United Aircraft introduced me to a multitude of contractors and suppliers who helped me out and gave me a chance. Jean-Guy Brosseau did the excavation so we could put in the foundation. My brother-in-law, Robin Graham, did the plastering. Perico, a company in Longueuil, financed all of the material when I couldn't afford to pay for it. Ralph Marrion helped with labor, as did Regis Lemieux.

When I was working at Northern Electric, Regis worked in the stall next to mine, and quickly became one of my best friends. His help was instrumental in constructing the apartments, coming to work during any spare time he had. Even my mother helped out, coming over every day after the workers had left to clean the place up. Not that we had a lot of workers. Usually it was just me, putting a few hours whenever I wasn't working at United Aircraft or Canada Packers. I sacrificed a lot to build what I believed would be a better future for my family. I was not often present for them during these times, but I always provided for them. None of it was easy.

This was around the time I was training to obtain my black belt status from the Canadian Kodokan Black Belt Association. As you get to the higher belts, you don't just need to demonstrate your knowledge, you need to win competitions in order to advance.

One such fight was against Terry Farnsworth. It wasn't necessarily spectacular at the time, I just eliminated him with a strangulation technique and won the match. What made the fight memorable is that years later, Terry won Canada's first Olympic Gold Medal in Judo. I was very fortunate to have had the opportunity to compete with him, and when you think of it, I literally beat the world champion in Judo!

The fight for my own black belt happened at the Maurice Richard Arena in 1968. My opponent was Charles Maingon. I watched a few of his previous matches during the competition, so I knew he was going to try to get me with a sieo nage – a shoulder throw. As soon as he attempted to throw me, I jumped over his shoulder and took him down with a strangulation technique – my favorite. When the official yelled "Hipo", I nearly had tears in my eyes.

I was shocked beyond words when they gave the fight to Maingon. I felt ashamed and heartbroken. Even the officials realized it was a bad call, but they could not reverse it.

For seven years, I had been pouring my heart and soul into judo, training whenever I could, and prioritizing it in my already overwhelmingly busy life. After this supposed defeat, I just couldn't do it anymore. The officials eventually realized they'd made a bad call, and awarded me an honorary black belt, but it was too little, too late. I still hold wonderful memories from my years of Judo, but I never competed after that. I kept going to the YMCA, but mostly focused on volleyball and scuba diving lessons instead.

THE FOLLOWING YEAR, we sold our house on Laurier street and moved into the newly finished apartment building on Holmes Street. It had eight bachelor apartments, while the main floor would be our new residence. I assumed I was going to live there for the rest of my life, so I built it to last forever, maintenance-free. It had super insulated walls, eighteen inches thick. In addition to the wooden frame, I used cement blocks filled with zonolite, and an exterior of stone and bricks. I used terrazzo for the stairs and hallways, and added a sauna bath, as well as a sun deck on the roof. It was meant to be paradise, so I even gave myself an insulated and heated garage. For the kids, I added a playhouse in the backyard, complete with bunkbeds and toys.

Our Apartment Building on Holmes.

We were so down to the wire with construction, that while the apartments were meant to be furnished, our tenants moved in on July 1st with nothing but the promise that the furniture was coming. It was an incredibly stressful time.

We had moved in a couple of months earlier, to get things ready, on May 1st 1969. I remember the date because my brother-in-law, Bruce, helped us with the move. While we were carrying my very heavy bedroom set on the stairs, Bruce somehow broke his back. For months after, he had to lie flat on his back, hang on doors, and all kinds of therapies of the day. He still suffers from it, over fifty years later. I felt so responsible and guilty, that I was very much a killjoy whenever anyone tried roughhousing around me, or anything that might bring a second back injury to my conscience.

To help ease the financial burden of constructing the apartment building, I convinced Barb to participate in what I now know was a pyramid scheme. We began selling a line of skincare products called Koscot, which stood for Kosmetics for the Communities of Tomorrow. Although it required a 5000$ investment, you got your money back as long as you recruited one other person to sell the products. In order to recruit someone, you had to pay for them to attend an information session at a fancy hotel in Montreal. Barb completed a training program, so she could do the demonstrations, while I worked on recruitment.

I did get my 5000$ for recruiting another poor soul, but I spent so much money sending people to the information sessions, and buying all of the products I was supposed to sell, that I ended up losing roughly 5000$ from the venture. By the seventies, Koscot was out of business and tangled up in a legal mess, so I was glad all we lost was money. Koscot was not my first attempt to supplement our income by being a salesman, which is not really in my skill set. At one point, I was an Encyclopedia Britannica salesman, and I even tried selling Amana freezers and food plans. Thankfully, I got the message after Koscot and focused on businesses rather than schemes.

To make up for all of the stress and to celebrate being done with construction, Regis and I took our families on a vacation to New Brunswick. I discovered early on that vacations are something you need to take whether you have the money for them or not. I'm not saying you should go into debt and live a lavish life above your means, but every once in a while, you need to disconnect from your daily life and recharge.

Regis and Gail rented a tent-trailer, while I borrowed a twenty-two-foot travel trailer from a friend at work. I was much more experienced with driving now, with my own cars as well as trucks and heavy equipment, but it was my first time pulling a travel trailer.

I don't remember much from the actual vacation. My most vivid memory from the trip is the drive home. While we were driving in the mountains, I was nearly falling asleep, but there was nowhere to pull off. In hindsight, this was a terrible idea and I do not recommend it, but Barb and I decided to switch drivers while we were still driving. Or rather, I decided, and Barb did as she was told. We managed the switch, but my trailer started to fish-tail, so we ended up with the trailer nearly hanging off the edge of a very deep cliff. I saw this and my heart stopped, as Barb and I rushed to get the kids out of the back seat. The trailer was still attached to our Buick Wildcat, but I somehow managed to unhitch it before the trailer plummeted down the cliff. It was so deep that we couldn't even see the trailer anymore, and couldn't salvage anything. I bet the trailer is still down there, but at least my family is safe.

The rest of the trip home was far from pleasant. I had to figure out how to tell my co-worker I lost his trailer. In the end, the trip cost a lot more than expected, as I had to pay him the entire cost of the trailer, which I later found out, he also claimed from the insurance company. Needless to say, I never borrowed expensive things from friends again.

II

BAR-B-DELIGHT

9

"If you can dream it, you can achieve it."
-Zig Ziglar

In 1970, the Quebec Government attempted to separate from Canada so they could form their own country. This still hasn't happened, but a tremendous amount of English businesses moved to other provinces and countries as a result.

My dream had always been to have my

own business, so this was a perfect opportunity to look for bargains these companies left behind. I was always one to follow my dreams, and as Wayne Gretzky said, "You miss 100% of the shots you don't take." So, I found a piece of commercial land on Taschereau boulevard and made a ridiculous offer. They were asking for 7$ per square foot, and I offered 1$.

I was shocked when, within 48 hours, they accepted. I was also in a panic, because I never thought they would accept such a lowball number, and didn't actually have the money. To be honest, I was so terrified by what I had done that I asked Barbara to come to the notary with me, so she could refuse to sign the papers and cancel the deal. Surely if my wife said no, they wouldn't make me go through with the purchase?

Barb, who is my partner in everything and always supports me, knew that I was just letting my fear get in the way. She refused to get me out of it. She did say that I got myself into the mess, so it was up to me to get myself out of it, but I think that if I was really stuck, she would have done it. She just believed in me, even when I didn't.

I HAD a good job at United Aircraft, and the bank would have all the land as equity, so they gave me a mortgage and I became the owner of 70 000 square feet of prime real estate. I saw its potential, but looking at the land, all you could see was a large ditch with no access to the busy street it bordered. We had to drive up a bunch of side streets to get to it, which was not going to work for a business. We had a lot of work to do.

First of which was to decide what business I wanted to own. Although I got the land for a steal, the taxes were extremely high, and I needed to start making money as soon as possible if I wanted to keep it. One thing I could always bank on was that Barb was an excellent cook. At the time, ribs were really growing in popularity, but there was no restaurant that sold them on the South Shore. It just so happened that Barb had the most delicious rib recipe I'd ever tasted. We decided to open a restaurant called Barb-B-Delight Restaurant Incorporated, where we would serve ribs, chicken, and steak.

Bar-B-Delight during the construction phase.

Although we knew we were going to open a restaurant, we were still a long way from getting there. Preparing the land for use was in and of itself a long-term, complicated endeavor. I had an old boss from United Aircraft, Jacques Bissonnette, who left to start a consulting firm, Soprin. His mechanical engineers and architects drew up all of our plans. I never would have been able to achieve my dreams without him coming to my rescue.

Once we had the building permits, my work began. One of our permits was so that we could close down the highway, after we put in the pipes, to hook our land up to water and sewage lines. We had to dig up the land to put in the pipes, then level it with thousands of loads of earth. Luckily, a contractor I had worked with before, Broadway Paving, had a lot of earth that they usually had to pay to dump in specially designated municipal lots. They were a godsend, as was Regis, who put in long hours of labor to help me out. Together, he and I constructed the bar fridges and all the light fixtures.

My friend Paquin did all of our plumbing, while I was the project manager. I found contractors to do the work I couldn't do, and figured out whatever I could. I poured concrete, did our floors and built the roof. We had stone walls in some places, with a stucco finish in others, and had to order special beams with steel plates from British Columbia for the roof. I assembled them myself, but had to hire a crane to put them up, as they were ridiculously heavy. I almost lost my arm while guiding the crane, when it got stuck between a heavy roof truss and the wall.

I wasn't the only one who was injured during construction. Near the end of it, my son, Danny, wanted to help us put up the light fixtures on the trusses of the roof. This required him to cross the wooden planks we put between them. I warned him to be careful and move slowly, but before I knew what was happening, he had fallen through to the floor, roughly fifteen feet below. He made it out with nothing more than a broken arm, but it took so long for them to see us at the hospital, that they had to re-break it before they could put the cast on.

IT WAS while we were building the restaurant that Guy Rouellan and I launched a Judo club at United Aircraft's Recreation Club. I was spending so much time on construction when I wasn't working, that I needed to be able to work out during my lunch breaks, or I wouldn't be able to work out at all. Plus, we thought a lot of the other men would enjoy it, and Guy was an amazing teacher. He was a big, tough guy who easily could have killed me, yet he let me throw him around in those classes, before I finally received my honorary black belt in 1972.

On the evening of August 29th, 1971, my dad came over and pounded on my door in a panic, saying my mom was very sick. By this point she was already bedridden, so it wasn't news, but the look on his face told me this was worse than anything she had faced before. He thought she might have had a heart attack, and wanted me to bring my oxygen tanks over while he waited for the doctor to come. I was taking scuba diving lessons, so I grabbed my tank and rushed over. I tried my best to revive her any way I could, but it was to no avail.

She died in my arms of a massive heart attack, after having been there for me my entire life. I suddenly understood the pain Barb had gone through when she lost her mother years earlier, as I felt like I couldn't breathe. My mother had done so much for us. She was kind and loved by everyone, but I don't know if she knew how much I loved her, or what she meant to me. Looking back now, fifty years after losing her, I still have her picture on my desk, and look at it every day. I miss her so very much. One of my biggest regrets is that I never got to spoil her for all that she did for us, and all of the sacrifices she endured so we would never be without.

THE FUNERAL WAS a blur of sad faces and tears, but there was physical pain in my chest as I had to wrestle Linda from the coffin when she insisted she wanted to give her grandmother one last hug. It broke my heart, because I wanted that last hug just as much as she did.

. . .

ROBERT WYNGAERT

My mother's death was the proverbial straw that broke the camel's back. Up to that point, I was soldiering through, from United Aircraft to the restaurant construction to Canada Packers, trying to fit in Barb and the kids. I had also taken up part time work as a Gentleman Bouncer for Garda, providing security at various sporting events, and being a first line bodyguard for special guests like Robert Bourassa (the Prime Minister of Canada) and Colonel Sanders (of KFC fame). All of this to keep our heads above water, but I was sinking. Barb and I both were, because the more responsibilities I took on outside of the home, to build my career and my dreams, the more Barb had to handle at home, in addition to her full-time job, like maintaining the two apartment buildings. The busy-ness had kept us from noticing that we were burning out, but my mother's death brought it all crashing down.

We went to see a doctor, figuring he could prescribe us something, or tell us we were being ridiculous and to suck it up. Instead, he shocked us both by saying we were experiencing burnout, and needed to take a vacation.

WE HAD LET GO of Mrs. Drummond months before, since the kids were all in school. With no regular babysitter, we asked Suzanne Leduc, a woman who lived in our apartment building, to mind the children while Barb and I took my brand-new Chrysler 300 and drove to Florida.

It was our first trip with just the two of us since the honeymoon, and I don't think either of us realized how much we needed it until we were gone. We stopped in Fort Myers to visit Ken Bloxham and his wife, Marge, then continued on to Walt Disney World. I particularly enjoyed the Thomas

Edison Museum we visited as well, but obviously, nothing can beat Disney. Barb was enjoying the trip a lot more before she got heat stroke, right about the time Suzanne called to tell us the children were not behaving. So we cut our trip short.

BY 1972, the Restaurant was built, so we applied for a liquor license before buying and installing all of the equipment. Pretty soon, we were ready to open, but still waiting on our liquor license. We were told that our request was under review, but we had invested every cent we had into this venture, and needed to start making money soon. We had a government representative handling our case, but after contacting him a few times to find out what was going on, he said that he was going through some personal finance problems. If we lent him some money, he would make sure our request went to the top of the pile. You hear rumors about governments being corrupt, but we quickly learned that the only way to get what we wanted was to grease their pockets.

Unfortunately, all of my money was tied up in the restaurant. I had even sold one of my apartment buildings to afford all of the construction. I asked how much he needed, and he told me five thousand dollars should get him out of his troubles. I went to my brother, Roger, who owned an Appliance store, and asked if I could borrow the money from him, explaining how desperate I was. Luckily, my brother agreed.

Caving in to his demands was clearly a terrible idea, as we found out less than a month after paying him off. This time, he told us that if we gave another five thousand dollars, his supervisor would sign off on the permit. I was so angry, both at him and at myself. I never laid a hand on him, but I came close. He knew it was taking all of my self-restraint not to take my anger out on him.

The inside of Bar-B-Delight.

In the end, Bar-B-Delight was open for nine months before we finally got our liquor license. During that time, it was very hard to get customers and keep the business open. People were reluctant to come in, even though our prices were reasonable, because the building was so fancy and luxurious that it scared them away. Once we did convince people to come inside, a lot of them would find out we didn't serve alcohol and either leave or never come back.

THE RESTAURANT WAS TRULY a family affair. Barb's father was in charge of the ribs and chicken, which he would sometimes have to prepare in the middle of the night, in the basement, terrified of every unidentified noise.

Danny would help him out, sometimes even manning the fort on his own, while Linda would clear the tables with her friend Sonia Keleman.

Bobby, Barb's brother, was our cook, who stayed with us from the day we opened to our very last day in business, even though he was more than qualified to be a professional chef anywhere else.

Barb would spend her days making the desserts, then become our waitress in the evenings. She sometimes acted as a barmaid, but hated working down in the basement, so we tried to avoid that.

My sister Irene, and Barb's sister Carole, were our friendly waitresses who kept the customers coming back. Irene's daughter, Francine, would often help out as well, running to get me whenever a customer tried to leave without paying.

Barb's brother Ronnie did the breakfast shifts, until we realized it wasn't financially profitable for us to be open for breakfast, so he did deliveries for a while.

Though she wasn't involved in the day-to-day operations, Barb's sister Joan spent hours washing and ironing all of our tablecloths so we could continue to deliver a five-star service.

My dad would even rent out the restaurant at Christmas to host a big Wyngaert Christmas Family Party with his new wife, Antoinette.

As for myself, I was the host most nights, and I handled all the deliveries, the inventory, the orders, and anything that fell through the cracks.

On Saturday nights, Georges, Denise, Barb and I would go to local restaurants, to check out the competition. It was nice to revive our old tradition, as we used to all go out together on Saturday nights when the kids were little. Whenever I saw something other restaurants were doing that seemed to be successful, I would try to think of how we could implement it at Bar-B-Delight.

Georges had moved out of my parents' duplex a few years before, and one of his new neighbors was a man named Michel Blanchard. Mike was incredibly well-known in the community, as he got involved in everything. He was a retired RCMP officer now working as a sales representative for Esso, an Alderman for the city, and he worked with me as my partner at Garda. Not to mention that he was the one who played the trumpet for the Montreal Canadiens hockey games, whenever a player scored a goal. He never explicitly worked for us, but he went out of his way to bring his coworkers there after a shift, or groups after a meeting…he was our unofficial advertising department, and we were incredibly grateful.

With our permit in hand, we quickly built a bar in the basement, hoping we could make up for the lost time, and revenue.

10

"Protecting yourself is self-defense. Protecting others is warriorship."
-Bodhi Sanders

Once we had our liquor license, we opened a bar in the basement section of the restaurant to increase our revenues. The restaurant itself wasn't enough to cover our expenses, and while the bar did help, it also brought a lot of problems. It is common sense that alcohol can bring out the worst in people, but I never realized how many stupid things people do when they drink, until I owned a bar.

We had an organ player and entertainers, trying to keep up with our classy theme, but that is not how things always played out.

For instance, we frequently had a professional wrestler, the Masked Destroyer, who would come to the restaurant. He was on a weekly wrestling program on television, and believed this gave him the right to eat and drink without ever paying his bill. He took advantage of his fame, insisting that he was bringing in business for us just by being there, and handing out autographed pictures of himself. I usually gritted my teeth and let it slide, but on this particular night, I'd spent the day working as a Gentleman bouncer for the Montreal

Expos. A double-header game. I arrived at the restaurant and found him there. Again. Eating and drinking things he would never pay for.

I waited until he went down to the bar in the basement, then confronted him about his bill. He told me not to mess with him, bragging about what he did to the last restaurant owner who 'challenged' him.

I'd had enough of his arrogance, of working so many jobs, of the restaurant not making money…I couldn't take it anymore.

"Let's see who destroys who," I said, taking off my jacket.

I'm not proud of what came next, but after our 'altercation' he left and never came back. I don't think he wanted the media to know that a professional wrestler was beat up for taking advantage of a small business owner. It very easily could have gone the other way, but it wouldn't have painted him in a good light if he'd beat me up either.

. . .

It goes without saying that I never used my martial arts training to provoke people, and I never took advantage of my abilities. I always relied on my skills solely as an insurance policy, to be used in defensive situations, to protect myself and others from injury. Most of them had to do with my business ventures, like renting bachelor apartments – one of them in a low-income area where collecting rents was not always easy, the restaurant, and the bar. I always made sure that I was physically fit, to ensure that our clients were safe in our establishments, and my family never had to worry.

11

"The only person you are destined to become is the person you decide to be."
-Ralph Waldo Emerson

A few months after we opened the restaurant, I was working as a gentleman bouncer at an Expos Games when Gilles Desormeaux, my supervisor, told me there was a scout looking for 'tough guys' who could pass as police officers in a new movie called The Pyx. We both auditioned, and it just so happened that the night the scout was there, a fight broke out at the game, and I had to break it up. Apparently, the scouts came to see us because their scene would show a bar fight being broken up by police officers. I guess I looked like I knew what I was doing, because I was chosen to play Detective Clement in the film.

One thing I have learnt about the film world is that things often change. The bar fight I was supposed to break up never happened. Instead, they told me I would be getting shot and falling off a boat. I said that was fine, picturing my father's fishing boat. On the day we were supposed to film that scene, I arrived to see a gigantic ship in the St. Lawrence River. Thank God the current was too strong to film the scene that way, because I do not think I would have been able to survive a fall into the water from that height, even if there was no current. Instead, I fell to the deck, and they put out a pile of boxes for the others to fall onto. The guns and other weapons are also fake, but the fire that comes out to make them look real could definitely injure someone.

Newspaper Clipping for The Pyx: Me, Christopher Plummer, Don Pilon, and Gilles Desormeaux.

The movie had some big names, like Karen Black, Donald Pilon, Yvette

Braind'amour, Jean-Louis Rioux and Christopher Plummer. Mr. Plummer was such a nice guy. He would eat and hang out with us, talking like we were his friends rather than starstruck dayplayers. He even asked me for some pointers on a scene where he had to punch someone, knowing I had a lot of experience in that area. I was so sad to hear of his passing, just as I finished writing this book.

At the end, I was invited to the wrap party, where all of the cast celebrated the end of the film shoot. It was really fun meeting all of these important people, after such an unexpected and exciting experience.

I WAS LATER CALLED to audition for another film, called Child Under a Leaf. It was once more for the part of a policeman, but I turned it down. I was already stretched so thin as it was, and my wife and children were more important to me than possibly pursuing an acting career. I was very happy with my position at United Aircraft and didn't want to jeopardize it, or the benefits it came with. I never regretted that decision.

I did, however, regret telling all of my friends and family to watch The Pyx when it came out the following year. The film was called The Hooker Cult Murders in other markets, which gives a better idea of what it is about. I especially got a lot of phone calls from the parents of children who went to school with mine, wondering why my children had told theirs to watch a movie with so much murder and nudity.

12

"Character cannot be developed in ease and quiet. Only through experience of trial and suffering can the soul be strengthened, ambition inspired, and success achieved."
— Helen Keller

Not long after we opened the restaurant, the hourly workers at United Aircraft Technologies went on strike, requesting higher pay and more benefits. In addition to striking, they frequently burnt police cars and vandalized the homes of some supervisors. They eventually settled after twenty-two months, but it was a very scary time for anyone associated with United Aircraft.

I was a salaried employee, so the strike didn't apply to me, but I was told that if I didn't come in, I would no longer have a job. Since my job entailed supervising the work of others, when the hourly workers stopped coming in, I had to cover for them.

I couldn't afford to lose my job, so I took on the responsibilities of all the employees under me. Or at least the ones that I knew how to do. Pratt hired scabs, and some supervisors went so far as to smuggle them into the plant with their personal vehicles, to protect them from the strikers. I know a lot of people were calling me a scab, but I didn't bring in anyone new, I just worked a lot of extra hours and did a lot of additional tasks for my same salary.

I was one of the only supervisors who held a class one driver permit, so I was assigned to drive the heavy equipment for snow removal, as well as transferring parts and equipment to other plants. When the strikers set fire to the warehouse where United Aircraft stored the casting and engine parts in Montreal, I was also the only one crazy enough to risk my life driving an eighteen-wheeler from the warehouse to our plants.

In urgent situations like that, they picked me up in a helicopter at the helipad in front of Plant #5 and brought me to Plant #1, because there was no way I was getting through the picket lines with my car.

Claude Labelle, me, and Guy Rouellan.

It was still extremely dangerous, so the Security team asked me what kind of protection I needed. Instead of one of the security guards, I asked for my Judo instructor, Guy Rouellan, to accompany me. He had black belts in both Judo and karate, so I knew he would have my back. They also decided that we should wear a wire, so they could monitor our activities, and send help if it was needed, as we didn't have cell phones at the time. They would have sent us with a police escort instead, but tensions were high, and it didn't make sense to endanger more lives and possibly escalate the situation if it wasn't necessary.

On one of those days, we were driving along Chambly road to bring a load of engine parts to Plant #5. When we stopped at a stop sign, I looked around and saw we were surrounded by pick-up trucks filled with angry strikers, and goons looking for a fight. We alerted the police over the wire, but weren't sure what to do while we waited. We could have stayed inside the truck until they got close enough to cause damage, at which point we would be trapped. We'd seen the pictures of police cars up in flames, and it looked like the men outside were angry enough to want to put us out of commission, so we didn't want to risk it.

I suggested we go outside and stand back to back so we could protect each other, and possibly come up with an escape plan. I acted confident, but I was terrified.

As soon as we got out, one of the strikers yelled, "It's Bob and Guy!"

Some still looked upset, but the majority stepped back, and convinced the others to as well. Our reputations were well known around the plants, so they knew we had no choice but to drive the truck, or we would lose our jobs. It was a tremendous sign of their respect for us, and we both greatly appreciated it. By the time the police arrived, we were the only ones there.

ONE DAY, I was assigned to cover for one of my millwrights to assemble a steel structure from an overhead bridge crane. While I was trying to secure a steel beam into place, the beam slipped and fell towards my supervisor. Without thinking, I moved to push it out of the way, so it wouldn't hit anyone, and fell to the concrete floor twenty feet below.

Everyone rushed to help me, but I got up on my own, amazing them all. This is one more time that it was a miracle I did not die. Perhaps it was because of all the break falls we practiced in my judo training, or that my mission on earth wasn't over yet.

Although I kept assuring everyone I was fine, I was actually in a lot of pain, so I went to my car and drove to see my chiropractor. By the time I parked, the pain was excruciating, and I could barely make it into his office.

After he took some x-rays, he told me it wasn't humanly possible for me to have driven myself in the condition I was in. My whole spine was completely out of line, with four vertebrae needing adjustments. He told me I was very fortunate to be in such good physical shape, because my muscles must have supported my spine and kept it in place while I drove there. He recommended that I take some time off to help with the healing process, a few months at least. I took his advice in the sense that I resigned from Canada Packers, after fourteen years of being one of the Brown Brothers, but I am very stubborn, so I was back at United Aircraft after a week.

13

"If you don't build your dream, someone else will hire you to help them build theirs."
-Dhirubhai Ambani

By July of 1974, I was risking my life for a company while my own business was falling through the cracks, so I made the difficult decision to resign from United Aircraft and devote myself full-time to Bar-B-Delight.

Because of the strike, local restaurants had been warned not to serve or deliver food to anyone still working for United Aircraft. Or for Garda, who was hired to protect the facilities from the strikers. Our restaurant was so close to bankruptcy, and I was already on the strikers' bad list because I drove the trucks, so I offered to supply all the meals United Aircraft and Garda needed, as long as they were the ones who came to pick the orders up. They agreed and gave us a purchase order that lasted until the end of the strike. It was a godsend. Our lifeline to keep the business running. My family and employees were kept very busy, and we received a monthly cheque that covered our operating expenses.

However, we were constantly on edge due to the many death threats we received from the strikers. They went so far as to call and say they were going to blow up the restaurant, with everyone inside it. Barb, who usually answered the phone, was a terrified pack of nerves. One time, I was the one who picked up, and happened to recognize the voice of the person threatening us. I called him by his name and told him I would hold him personally responsible if anything happened to the restaurant, my family, or any of my employees. He would have to deal with me, as well as the police. We never received another call.

I thought life would be easier and I would have more free time now that I was only managing the one business, without all of my other jobs. I didn't realize that owning a restaurant was 7 days a week, 365 days a year. Plus, you don't get paid by the hour, you get paid if you make it profitable. I didn't have the money to hire all of the personnel that would be required to run the restaurant I wanted ours to be, so I relied on my family to go above and beyond their tasks, knowing that I was paying them less than they deserved, or could be making other places. Everyone pitched in as needed. I know that I personally filled in as cook, barman, host, dishwasher, janitor, delivery man, restocking the kitchen and bar...it never ended.

14

"Every strike brings me closer to the next home run."

-Babe Ruth

Nine months after I resigned from United Aircraft, in February of 1975, the strike finally ended, almost two years after it began. Gordon MacCaul, the plant superintendent, called me to see if I would consider returning to work for them at the newly-named Pratt & Whitney Canada. He knew I was busy with the restaurant and probably couldn't do it, but he offered me the position of General Foreman at Plant #2. This was a position I had been hoping to get for years, but every time there was a vacancy, I was passed over because I didn't have the basic qualifications – meaning an Engineering Degree or an M.B.A.

I agreed and went back, letting him think I was doing them a favor, without ever letting on how desperate I had been to return to work. I am sure their offer would have been much less if they had known.

While returning to Pratt gave me the job I wanted and opportunities to further my education through job-related courses, it also meant leaving Barb with all of the responsibilities of the restaurant, the bar, and the children.

This was too much for her, so we hired a manager to look after the bar. We chose Richard B., the man who sold us a lot of the kitchen equipment and other items for the restaurant. He was a young, retired policeman with a wife and four children. It seemed like a perfect match.

Danny and I in Florida.

In December, after a long and busy

summer, we needed a vacation. It was impossible with the restaurant, but Richard offered to manage Bar-B-Delight in its entirety while the family spent two weeks in Florida. It was such a relief to be able to travel all of us together, and leave our restaurant in the hands of someone we knew and trusted, who was intimately familiar with our business.

We flew to West Palm Beach just after Christmas. We had to leave extremely early in the morning, before the sun came up. I was used to flying because of Pratt, but it was the first flight for Barb and the kids. I know people these days wear comfortable clothes when they fly, but we got dressed up for it. And I don't just mean that we didn't wear our sweatpants; we went all out. Barb and the girls wore dresses, Danny had a nice vest, and I wore a suit, complete with an ascot tie. I didn't wear an ascot in my everyday life, but for some reason, I felt it was appropriate for plane rides. It seems so silly when I look back on it now, but at the time, we took it all very seriously.

We stayed at the Colonnades Hotel and I rented a brand new, light blue 1976 Cadillac Sedan. I liked the car so much, that I bought one for myself when I got home. The hotel was really something, with a staircase and two floors contained within our room.

We brought the kids to Walt Disney World and the Thomas Edison Museum, went on tours of the swamps to look for gators, we picked oranges…it was a lot of fun.

When we returned from the trip and went to check on things at the restaurant, tanned and refreshed to get back to work, we found it all boarded up. I was in denial, giving Richard the benefit of the doubt, telling myself there had to be a logical explanation. It wasn't until we went inside and saw that all of our equipment was gone, down to the dining room chairs, that I faced the truth. While we were on vacation, the man we trusted to manage our business had betrayed us, selling all of our equipment and closing up shop. I wondered if that was how he got the equipment when he sold it to us in the first place.

I went to his home to confront him, but we weren't the only ones he betrayed. He had purchased a motorhome with the money, then left his wife and kids behind when he disappeared. She was broken-hearted and had no idea where he was.

YEARS LATER, his wife contacted me after finding out he was living in an apartment in Longueuil. She gave me the address and his apartment number, so I could pay him a visit. He was shocked when he opened the door and found me, but I took advantage of his surprise to push my way inside. He ran to his bedroom and came back with a handgun, that he brandished while accusing me of forced entry.

"If you don't leave, there will be blood on the walls," he threatened.

I had long ago written it off as a bad debt experience, so I decided the money wasn't worth my life, and went home.

A FEW MONTHS LATER, I happened to see him in a restaurant, sitting at a table by himself. I assumed he wouldn't have the gun on him, and if he did, he wouldn't dare use it, so I took a seat at his table.

He knew that without the gun, he wasn't going to get past me, so he told me that he would pay me back, and gave me twelve post-dated cheques of two thousand dollars each.

I was very happy with this deal. Although it would only cover about half of what he owed me, it was better than the nothing I had been expecting. The first two cheques went through before he closed his accounts, and we never heard from him again.

III

CAMPING ALOUETTE

15

"Opportunity is often missed because it comes dressed in overalls and looks like work."
-Thomas A. Edison

Since reopening the restaurant would have required purchasing all new equipment and furnishings, for a business that was not profitable to begin with, we decided to cut our losses and sell it. Earlier, when trying to make ends meet, I had already sold off parts of my land to Kentucky Fried Chicken. This time, we sold to Rotisseries St-Hubert, but they only wanted the land. This meant we had to pay to demolish the restaurant we poured our hearts and souls into. I made a deal with a contractor so he did it for free in exchange for whatever materials they could salvage.

I settled into my position at Pratt, and Barb went to work at Kapetan, a local restaurant. It broke my heart, but it was also a relief, as our restaurant had been a failure, financially speaking.

People who met me later in life know me as a successful business man, and would probably call me well-off, but that's because they never saw all the struggles it took to get me there. I spent most of my life working multiple jobs, trying any additional income streams I could find, failing time and time again at new business ventures before I 'made it'. When the kids were born, I took out a life insurance policy, that would pay off all my debts if I died. I told them the more debt I had, the richer they would be. The truth was that I believed in investing in yourself and your future. It stung, but I would rather go into debt trying to improve myself and provide for my family, than to scrape by without ever even trying to do better. Luckily, every failed attempt was a stepping stone, teaching me lessons so I would be prepared when the opportunity came.

IN MAY, Ken Bloxham called to see if I was interested in purchasing shares in his campground. Their permit to have it on the airstrip had expired, and they were now located in Saint-Mathieu-de-Beloeil, having purchased Camping Beloeil, that had been about to file for bankruptcy. He heard about us closing the restaurant, and wondered if I would want to invest in Kendan Ltd.

Years ago, I had tried to purchase a campground with Barb's cousin, Ray Bonin. We had even gone so far as to give a 5000$ deposit, but the owner died and the deal fell through. Ken's offer was my second chance, but at this point in my life, I had no intentions of starting a new business. The restaurant had discouraged me, and I was resigned to just keep working at Pratt until I could retire. However, my accountant had warned me that the best way to avoid being taxed for Capital Gains was to invest in something new, so I didn't say no. Ken suggested I come work there for the summer, as a trial, but also so they could train me.

I no longer worked at Canada Packers, so I spent my nights and weekends at the campground instead. I worked hard, long hours, and remember being surprised by how little they were investing in the property. They held meetings to see if they should replace faulty doorknobs, which often led to me purchasing small items on my own, so I wouldn't have to deal with the meetings. Their mindset, which I later found out is very common, was to keep going with minimal investment, as long as they were making a return. My mindset, on the other hand, was to keep investing the returns back into the business, building it up to its full potential.

This was 1976, when Montreal built the Olympic Stadium to host the Summer Olympics. We happened to be the closest campground to Montreal, which meant we got a lot of business and the company made a fortune. Before the start of the next summer I put everything I had, 130 000$, into purchasing a third of the shares of Kendan Ltd.

. . .

THAT SUMMER, I put Barb and the kids to work from May to October. It was my second year at the campground, but my first as part-owner. Barb took the summer off from working at Kapetan to run the office, though she also found herself doing whatever was needed. Linda left her job at Roger's ice cream shop in order to help Barb out in the office. Sandra was heartbroken to have to stop babysitting Bobby and Moe's daughters; Karen, Donna, and Kathy. Her new job was taking care of visitors. We didn't have a gate at the time, so if the visitor didn't stop to register with her, she would have to chase them down through the park. Danny wasn't allowed to leave his job cutting the grass at our apartment building, but he got the added responsibility of helping out with the campground's maintenance, especially on weekdays, when I couldn't be there.

. . .

UNBELIEVABLE BUT TRUE

We were only in charge of the campground, as the previous owners still ran the general store, the snack bar, and the arcade. We had 250 sites, and rented them for 5.50$ per night, with the option of electricity, water, and sewage for 0.50$ each.

Now that I was part-owner, Ken and Dan became more like silent partners. They handled the accounting and stopped by occasionally to see how things were going, and to guide us as to what needed to be done, but they had very minimal involvement in the day to day operations. Most of the grounds work went to Jean-Marc Leblanc, who did everything from grass and repairs, to plumbing and electricity.

When I was able to be there, mainly nights and weekends, one of the campers, ten-year-old Marco Bissonnette, followed me around like he was my shadow. When people asked who he was following, he would tell them I was his father. We both had dark features, so I think they believed him, although I hope his father never heard him say that. I don't know if he was interested in learning how to run a campground, or if it was just something for him to do, but he went everywhere with me.

THE OTHER OWNERS didn't want to invest any money into the campground, so I did what I could to improve it without spending too much on capital expenditures. Danny and I leveled sites, Barb painted picnic tables...I had big plans, and slowly but surely, I would make them come true.

By the end of the summer, Sandra and Linda loved their new jobs, as they were able to sunbathe when we didn't have customers, which was often. It was good for their tans, but very bad for business.

OVER THE WINTER, I spent my evenings taking business administration and microeconomics classes at Champlain College. All of my entrepreneurial endeavors had been failures up to that point, teaching me many lessons, but I thought it might be nice this time to learn in a classroom, rather than from my own mistakes.

16

"Think of adversity as an opportunity for growth."
-Unknown

Unfortunately, a series of external factors worked to ensure the campground would have terrible attendance rates, as well as revenues, for the first few years after I became a partner.

When Canada switched to the metric

system, they had to change all of the exit numbers on the highway, to reflect their distance in kilometers rather than in miles. We had no warning of when this was going to happen, so we had already printed all of our promotional materials for the year when exit 64 switched to exit 105. All of our non-regular campers came in complaining about how hard it was to find us. Thank God for a Jehovah's Witness convention that nearly sustained our entire summer by bringing twelve thousand dollars in revenue.

In the fall of 1978, Iranian workers had gone on strike and the U.S. deregulated oil prices, which led to oil rationing and shortages. It didn't affect Quebec as much as the States, where people had to line up for hours to fill their cars, but we were part of an industry that catered to tourists. With the high prices and long wait times for gas, very few people wanted to travel long distances. Especially not towing a trailer.

Still, low attendance did not mean that we got to slack off. A lot of the work needed to be done whether we had campers or not, so it was becoming difficult to manage the apartment building and the campground. We made a decision and put our home on Holmes for sale in 1979, including the furniture, since we advertised furnished apartments. I thought everyone would be happy to get all new furniture in the new house, but Linda and Sandra were very upset with me for quite some time, as their bedroom set had belonged to my mother.

We purchased a new house at 411 Tailhandier in St-Bruno, on the mountain. It was a beautiful, large house on a corner lot, but it didn't have a garage. I had grown used to, and slightly dependent on my heated garage, so I drew up plans and got to work building myself one before the campground got busy.

Since we were adding a garage, I figured we would also add an extra bedroom above it, instead of wasting the space. I even planned a circular, paved driveway in the front of the house, and a double driveway on the side, so we could accommodate ten cars.

I had just finished all the framework when a building inspector came to visit us. We showed him what we were doing, and he told us we had to stop construction immediately. Apparently, there was a new by-law that made it unacceptable to put rooms above garages. I could either lower the structure so it couldn't be used as a living space or tear the whole thing down. I was not happy, but I had no choice but to comply.

17

"Always do your best. What you plant now, you will harvest later."
-Og Mandino

I was doing very well at Pratt, continuously finding ways to improve how things were done, and taking as many courses as the company made available to me. My abilities also improved every time they entrusted me with more responsibilities.

Unfortunately, Pratt soon found out that I was the owner of a campground, which they considered a conflict of interest. I had always had another job, or business, almost the entire time I was working for them. After the restaurant, the apartment buildings, and Canada Packers, I found it interesting that the campground was where they drew the line. Luckily, I was only part-owner, so I assured them we shared the responsibilities and it wouldn't be an issue. They asked me to sign a statement ensuring that the running of the campground would not interfere with my position and responsibilities at Pratt. It was also implied that I would be closely monitored, and wouldn't be able to take days off unless I was deathly ill.

Pratt & Whitney clearly had nothing to

worry about however, as I was presented with the United Technologies Award for Extraordinary Management Effectiveness in 1981.

18

"What you put into life is what you get out of it."
-Clint Eastwood

My first three years at the campground, our revenues were so bad, in fact, that Ken and Dan informed me that they would be filing for bankruptcy. For them, my investment had been a last-ditch attempt to salvage the company, but after a series of bad years, it was time for them to throw in the towel. For me, I had just invested every cent I'd made from selling the restaurant into this business, that they basically wanted to throw away. I had come into the camping business with high hopes, that I would work at Pratt until the campground became profitable, then I would retire and live out the rest of my life running a business that I could pass on to my children. I could see that we'd had a terrible couple of years, that it was a bad investment and I shouldn't have made it. But now that I had, I was not prepared to give up.

    I begged them to reconsider, before offering to buy them out. I couldn't buy all of their shares at once, but we came up with a payment plan, so I could slowly acquire more and more of the shares as time went on, ensuring they would get their money back.

ONE OF THE first things I remember doing is purchasing a tractor with money I earned from working at Pratt. Whenever something required equipment, Ken and Dan would always pay someone to bring their own and do the work. They were both engineers, who saw the campground as an investment, but I was someone who worked my way up in the world through construction, manual labor, and heavy lifting. I knew that it would be much less expensive in the long run if I had the equipment to do the work myself. If I didn't put money into the campground—a lot of it – I was going to lose it.

Sandra, Danny, me, and Linda in Jamaica.

THAT WINTER, to prepare for the demanding summer I knew was coming, we went on our first 'all-inclusive' vacation. It was a far cry from the ones we go on now. The resort was called Go Bananas and was located in Montego Bay, Jamaica. Instead of having to carry your money around with you, all of the prices were in bananas, which you would buy at the office and wear around your neck like a really long necklace. Any time you wanted something to eat or drink – or even a souvenir – you simply unhooked the required amount of bananas, then retied your necklace.

While we were there, we went to see Mico Blanco. He was the limbo king, who would lie planks of wood across rows of pop bottles, set the wood on fire, then limbo under the length of the wooden plank. It was very impressive!

Barb and I participated in all of the activities. It was hard not to, with the three children cheering us on. We won an award for our reggae dancing, but didn't do so well at Find Your Husband. The game consisted of blindfolding all the wives, then letting them find their husbands by feeling all of the men in the line, which included young studs as well as the husbands. I wouldn't exactly call myself a jealous guy, but I may have uttered a few 'Barb!'s under my breath when she lingered a little too long on the guy beside me.

As we were there over Christmas, they had a Jamaican Santa ride in on a surfboard. We also went carolling around the hotel, holding candles, which made it extra hilarious when our 'animator', Spike, fell into the pool. We watched all the shows from our balcony, bet on crab races, and even participated in the scavenger hunt, which had us looking for things like cockroaches. I think we purposely didn't find any.

It was a wonderful way to relax, recharge, and spend some time with the family.

19

"These tears need to be shed, wept into the earth where there is no hope of consolation. Sometimes a man has to cry alone."
-Edmond Manning

Joseph Wyngaert and Robert Thompson.

My father had been having a lot of heart problems, with almost daily angina attacks, but his surgery kept being delayed due to nursing strikes. We were thrilled when he was finally called for surgery on January 18th 1981, hoping this meant he would get back to his normal self. I was at home that evening when they told me that he had died on the operating table.

The surgery was delayed too many times, so by the time they got to him, it was already too late. These days, it isn't hard to get me emotional enough to shed a few tears. Just talking about how grateful I am for my family will do it. Back then I was much better at holding it all in. My kids could have counted on one hand the times they saw me cry, and they wouldn't need all of their fingers. This was one of those times, but I didn't want my children to see me like that, so I said I was going to work at the campground, and left so I could absorb the news on my own.

His death hit me differently than my mother's had, because my father was a very different person. My mother had been warm and generous with her love and affection, but my father was less demonstrative. He would often say 'you shouldn't talk to say nothing', so his words were few and far between. He was hard on me, and it wasn't always easy being his son, but I loved him, and I knew that he loved me. More than that, I knew that he loved Barbara, as he would often give Georges and I approving looks, saying we did good and were very lucky, whenever our wives were mentioned.

Danny, me, Barbara, and Sandra in Hawai'i.

Over the Christmas holidays, we went on a family vacation to Hawai'i. Even though we paid an arm and a leg for the direct flight, it still took us twelve hours to get there. Luckily, the unforgettable experience we had over the next two weeks made it well worth it.

We stayed at the Hyatt Regency, where we would sit by the pool and drink fancy drinks like Mai Tais, Blue Hawai'is, and Piña Coladas. These were very expensive, but we worked so hard during the year that I refused to worry about money while we were on vacation.

One day, they were filming a TV show at our hotel. I had no idea who or what Magnum P.I. was, but the kids went crazy over him, wanting to spend the entire day watching them film. I insisted we go do some sightseeing, but they were lucky enough to get pictures with Tom Selleck before we left.

We attended many shows, including Don Ho and Jim Nabors, the Kodak show, as well as a luau, which was delicious. It was so impressive to see everything they do with fire. We also went on tours, such as to the Dole Pineapple Plantation, and on hiking adventures to the top of Diamond

Head Volcano. It was the first time I heard of chocolate dipped cockroaches, which were apparently quite the delicacy. Maybe that's why they had us hunting for them in Jamaica!

When we visited the North Shore, everyone except for Barb ignored the signs and walked along the beach, with the water barely up to our ankles. We knew how to swim, and it wasn't like the waves could be dangerous in such shallow water. Or so we thought.

In an instant, a giant wave came and carried us into the undertow. Danny and Sandra were carried out in the distance, so as soon as I caught my breath, I went after them.

Sandra was the youngest, so I went to her first, having to practically wrestle her to the beach. I hadn't realized that the wave ripped off her bathing suit, and she was mortified, begging me to let her die. It's hard enough to save someone who is drowning – because they flail and drag you down – but it is even harder when the person doesn't want to be rescued. By the time I got to Danny, he was already on the beach, not very happy with me for saving her first. Luckily, we were all okay.

On New Year's Eve, the tradition was to have fireworks, which we enjoyed at first, but they lasted all through the night, ensuring no one would be able to sleep through the festivities. It was a wonderful vacation, but very expensive.

20

"We cannot direct the wind, but we can adjust the sails."
-Aristotle

One of the first years at the campground, my brother Georges came to work for us part-time to help out. I knew from Canada Packers that he wouldn't enjoy working on the grounds, so he worked in the office with the girls. At the time, we kept track of reservations and which sites were rented by a rather large map we hung on a corkboard wall. Small pins meant the site was occupied, while reservations got a sewing pin with a sticker of the dates on it. The map was color-coded to reflect which sites had which services, and was made out of regular paper, which came in handy when we made modifications to the sites, but it probably wasn't the most durable system.

After the summer Georges worked for us, we had to print a whole new map. Every time a customer came in with a comment on their site, such as 'muddy', 'pothole', 'noisy' or 'shaded', he would write it on the map, in pen or in marker. It was useful to know if the site had lots of trees, or if we needed to repair something, but many of the comments were dependent upon the weather, or who was camping beside them.

There was a lot of trial and error in the beginning, as well as many attempts to drum up business and make money. I had to pay Ken and Dan every April for their shares, which was long before campers arrived for the summer, so I came up with a promotion where seasonal campers received a discount if they paid in full before leaving in the fall. I wouldn't have made it through those years without people like my brother-in-law Doug, my nephew Danny Smith, and my brother Roger lending me money to tide us over until the season picked up.

After years of Andre Mirreault, the old owner of Camping Beloeil, running the snack bar, the general store, and the arcade, we decided it was time for a change. Kids enjoyed the games, and we ate at the snack bar almost every day, but the store was a joke. The prices were ridiculously high, so the only people who shopped there were the unfortunate campers who hadn't brought a car to get into town. It was highway robbery.

I purchased all remaining assets of Camping Beloeil, a 70 000$ investment, but with a little revamping and fair prices, I was confident we could run the store at a profit. It came with a private residence, which I used as my private office. Since it had a bedroom, Barb and I also stayed there some nights in the summer, so we didn't have to drive back and forth to St-Bruno.

With the addition of a new gate at the entrance, visitors had to come inside the office to register, meaning that Sandra no longer had to run after them. We put her to work in the office, which was much busier now that it included the store and the snack bar. Not to mention everyone needing change for the arcade.

. . .

Soon after, I purchased the balance of the prime commercial land from Kendan Ltd. It was situated between the highway and the sites, so we thought it would be the perfect place to put a driving range for our campers. With the Vallée du Richelieu Golf Course so close, it sounded like a sure thing. Unfortunately, it was a $100,000 investment that did not produce a good return. Apparently, most campers are not golfers.

Instead of being discouraged, we tried again, purchasing fifteen acres of wooded land behind the campground. Our plan was to promote Army Paintball Games, which were quickly rising in popularity. It was a way for us to offer another activity for our clients, and to increase our revenues with very little investment on our part, other than the land. We hit a goldmine! Not only did the campers enjoy it, but locals came all the time, venturing down to our snack bar for lunch. It was good for everyone's business!

21

"What doesn't kill you, makes you stronger."
-Friedrich Nietzsche

On August 3rd 1982, I was working at Pratt when I felt sick. I went to the washroom and found blood in my stools. There'd been a bit in them the day before, and I had dropped a case of beer from feeling woozy, but this time there was a lot of blood. I didn't want to wait too long like

I had for the appendicitis, so I asked to have the rest of the day off and drove myself to the Montreal General Hospital. I parked haphazardly in front of the emergency doors and walked towards the entrance, but I passed out before I reached it.

When I woke up, they told me that I had a bleeding duodenal ulcer that had almost been fatal, and I was far from being out of the woods. I had already lost two-thirds of my blood over the past few days and needed transfusions and surgery immediately. They performed a gastrectomy, resecting my ulcer and saving my life. I could not believe that once more, the good Lord had decided to spare me.

I spent two weeks in the hospital, a week or so recovering, then went back to work. I told my secretary, Jeanette, how difficult it was for the employees to manage the campground office, the store, and the snack bar. I was contemplating getting rid of the snack bar, but that would mean our campers would have to drive over 10 kilometers to get to the nearest restaurant, Marie-Antoinette, in St-Hilaire. I was just sharing it as water cooler talk, but she offered to take it over with her daughter. We bought an old bus and moved all of the equipment into it so they could run the snack bar the following year.

22

"We do not stop working and playing because we grow old. We grow old because we stop working and playing."
-George Bernard Shaw

Danny Smith, Brenda, me, and Sandra in Myrtle Beach.

Often in the spring, to take advantage of the calm before busy camping seasons, Barb and I would take golfing trips to Myrtle Beach. The kids came occasionally, with Danny bringing his girlfriend, Liz, one year, and Sandra taking golfing lessons with us. We would also be joined by various other family members.

One year, we went with Danny Smith and his wife Brenda. We took my beautiful

Lincoln Continental Collector Series Limousine with a gold grille, which turned a lot of heads at work. Not just because it was a nice car, but it was the same one the United Aircraft president drove, so people would do double-takes to make sure I wasn't him.

We only stopped for gas and essentials, so with the four of us taking turns driving, we arrived in record time for days spent playing golf and lounging by the pool. On the last four days of our vacation, Barb's father met up with us, along with Ronnie, and a family friend named Cy. Ronnie, who missed Anne almost as soon as he arrived and wanted to go home early, was woefully surprised when we woke up to find Myrtle Beach covered in snow.

The locals acted like they had never seen such a thing, so overnight, everything was closed. Golf courses, restaurants, movie theaters, gas stations…everything. All we could do was hang out at the hotel. Our golf game didn't improve, but we still managed to have a great time with the excellent company.

23

"Ignoring things won't make them go away. It only makes it harder to face them when they finally come around."
-A. Meredith Walters

In 1984 I sold my Lincoln and downgraded to a Chrysler 5th Avenue for $20 000. Clearly, the prices of cars were going up! About three weeks after I bought it, I was driving to work at Pratt, heading West on Highway 20. I noticed the vehicle in front of me was pulling a fairly large trailer, and thought, 'you're going the wrong way'. It was my first thought whenever I saw campers driving away from our campground. It was only when the trailer got unhitched that I started to worry, but by then it was already coming right at me.

I applied the brakes, hoping I could avoid it, and sighed with relief when I stopped inches from the trailer. Unfortunately, the 18-wheeler in back of me failed to do the same. His breaks took longer to kick in, so he crashed into the back of my new car. My driver seat, which was bolted to the frame, broke off so that I ended up on the back seat.

I managed to free myself from the safety belt and got out of the car as bystanders rushed to help me. I told them I was fine, but I couldn't help staring at my car, that was totalled, with smoke coming out of it. I took a few steps back, just in case it decided to blow up, and waited for the authorities, trying to digest the fact that I had yet again been in a traumatic accident, and survived.

After the police got my version of what happened, the paramedics insisted I go to the hospital to get checked out. I refused, explaining that I felt fine, and was already late for work as it was. They were reluctant, but they couldn't hold me, so they let me go.

It just so happened that Barb was on her way home from an appointment when she drove by the accident and recognized our car, so she picked me up and drove me to work. I had to lie and tell her the paramedics had cleared me, or she would have brought me right to the hospital.

I truly felt fine and had no pain when I left the crash site that day, but in hindsight, I should have listened to the paramedics.

ONE EVENING THAT SUMMER, we had a very bad storm. There were high winds and heavy rain while the campground was at full capacity. We were having dinner as a family, like we did every Sunday, when the wind brought down the main power line that was feeding our 550-volt transformer, as well as the main panels that supplied power for the whole campground. It was impossible to get an electrician on a Sunday evening, so I asked Linda's fiancé, Daniel Cavanagh, to help me out. There were a lot of Dannys in our family, so we usually called him Cazzie.

I knew it was a dangerous task, but I couldn't reconnect the broken mainline by myself. I needed him to hold the wire while

I installed the birdie connector. As long as we were careful to not make contact with the other wires, or the steel pipe that was supporting the wires, we would be alright.

This was probably one of the stupidest things I have ever done in my life. I could have electrocuted myself, and my future son-in-law, getting us both killed. Thank God it worked out and the campground electricity was restored.

Linda and I on her wedding day.

Luckily, that risky night didn't deter Cazzie from joining the family. He and Linda got married on September 8th, 1984. I have to admit I shed a few tears watching my firstborn get married and leave the nest, but Cazzie was a great guy, from a good family, and I knew he would take care of her.

As for Barbara, while Linda was on her honeymoon, she played the Teddy Pendergrass CD nonstop, so she could listen to Hold Me, which was Linda's first waltz, and cry. She eventually got over it, but it took a while.

IN THE FALL, Barb and I took a trip to Myrtle Beach with Roger and Kay. I was using my newly replaced Chrysler, while Roger drove down with his motorhome. Almost as soon as we arrived, I started having excruciating pains in my right arm and the back of my neck, residual damage from my car accident months earlier. Still, I kept playing golf and going to the beach, not wanting to ruin anyone's vacation.

After a week or so, I could no longer stand the pain, so I went to see a chiropractor. I went to see him every day that week, but to no avail. Ultimately, he recommended that I return home and go straight to the hospital.

You might be noticing a theme here, of me ignoring my body when it tells me I am stressed, of working through pain, and recklessly endangering myself in the name of being tough and strong. I hope you are also noticing that simple things tend to get complicated and hit me a lot harder than they should.

We had to cancel the rest of our vacation and returned home, covering 1740 kilometers in 19 hours, which did not help my pain. We drove straight to the Montreal General Hospital's Emergency Room, but by then I was almost completely paralyzed on my right side.

I was admitted on November 2nd, and they soon performed a major surgery on my spine, specifically the R6 and R7 vertebraes, called the cloward procedure. It was very risky, as they removed pieces of bone from my hip, and cut my throat from ear to ear to get to the damaged vertebrae. They then placed the bones from my hip into my spine to secure it.

Even with the surgery a success, there was still a good chance I would be paralyzed, so I was advised not to move my head for 24-48 hours. They warned me that even in the best-case scenario, I wouldn't be able to rotate my head from side to side again. I would have to turn my whole upper body in order to look to my side. They considered it a minimum disability compared to having half of my body completely paralyzed, and I wholeheartedly agreed.

I waited until I was released to try and rotate my head. I did it very slowly at first, but continued doing daily head rotations, eventually regaining full mobility. I have kept it up to this day, over thirty years later.

Never doubt what determination can do.

UNFORTUNATELY, when I tried to bring my claim to the Société De l'Assurance Automobile, I was refused on the grounds that I didn't go to the hospital at the time of the accident, so they couldn't be sure that was when I got hurt. Upon release, I had a 7% loss of capacity on my right side, and there was nothing I could do about it. The only bright side was that it made me realize that all the money and power in the world cannot replace health. As they say, 'if you don't make time for your wellness, you'll be forced to make time for your illness', which I was.

24

"Success usually comes to those who are too busy to be looking for it."
-Henry David Thoreau

We were dealing with theft and vandalism, both at the campground, and at our house in St-Bruno. During the summer, Barb and I lived at the campground, and during the winter we were always in St-Bruno, leaving both homes unattended for extended periods of time. It was also getting busy at the campground, with the entire family travelling a half an hour each way after already working very long hours.

I figured it was about time that we sell the house in St-Bruno and move into the existing residence at the campground. We still had Sandra living with us, so I added a 40' X 40' extension to the existing residence, main office, and store. The only issue was that I only had forty days to design, plan, and implement the extension before the people who bought our house moved in. Not to mention the building permits.

It was no ordinary house that I designed, with three massive stone fireplaces; one in the dining room, one in the living room, and one in the garage. In addition to being able to fit all three of our cars, the garage would also be used as our recreation hall for parties. The campground was located in the suburbs, in an area that had many power failures during the winter months, and I didn't want my family to freeze. In addition, the building would house the washrooms, showers, and laundry facilities for the campers.

To achieve this almost impossible task of building the house in forty days, I had to use all of my skills from past experiences planning, scheduling and implementing. It also took all of my previous contacts, especially Paquin, without whom I never could have achieved it. I was stressed to my limit.

It required two shifts of tradesmen sixteen hours per day, seven days a week. Thank God I knew so many, but I still had to be on site to help them out, and to direct the project. Instead of traveling that year, I took my month of vacation time to see it through.

The house at the campground.

By July, the house was completed, and we were moved in. At Pratt, Royal Demers asked me to be in charge of his responsibilities as director of plant engineering while he took a week off. I was authorized to act on his behalf during this time. I was honored by the trust he put in me, and on cloud nine for the entire week he was gone. I couldn't help thinking of all the professional engineers and architects, or workers with MBAs and doctorate degrees that he passed up, choosing me instead.

THAT SUMMER, Linda took over the snack bar with Bobby. He already had a full-time job, so Linda was in charge of most of the day-to-day operations, with him bringing his daughter, Donna, to help almost every day. It was there that Donna would meet one of the campers, Dino Forbes, who would become her life partner, and the father of her two children. We were very sad to lose Linda in the office, but it was a godsend to have someone we trusted, who made delicious food, running our snack bar. I was proud that my daughter was following in my entrepreneurial footsteps of owning her own business.

. . .

In the Fall of 1985, Royal called me into his office to ask if I would consider taking a temporary position as Plant Superintendent. I would be replacing Gordie MacCaul until they found someone with the necessary qualifications to fill the position permanently. As in someone with an engineering degree.

Even though I knew it was way over my head, I accepted the position. My experience working with tradesmen and professionals in the past was certainly a big asset, as well as all of the courses I had been taking. I was continuously improving my education with Management Courses at Concordia, and even the Dale Carnegie course, which taught me so much about Public Speaking and relating to people in a professional capacity.

. . .

This was the first year Barb didn't have to work at Kapetan Restaurant in the winter. The campground was doing well enough that once the season ended, Barb was able to spend her winters looking after the campground, which was much less busy. She deserved it after the crazy hours we worked all summer.

25

"Don't let schooling interfere with your education."
-Mark Twain

It took until 1986 for Pratt to find a qualified replacement for the Plant Superintendent. The man they chose, Yves Lachambre, was a brilliant mechanical engineer I had worked with before. He had the charisma of a leader, was career-driven, and had the ability to achieve success. I was sad to leave the position, but it couldn't have gone to a better man, and I was glad to work with him.

His promotion meant that his previous position as Senior General Supervisor was up for grabs, so I took on his responsibilities at Plant #1 and reported to him. I was receiving a lot of attention for filling in for and temporarily replacing senior management, but these 'promotions' never lasted. I had the knowledge and the experience to do the job, but I was lacking the required degrees to hold on to them once suitable candidates were found.

I had just been passed over for a permanent position, yet again, when Alex Gilliland, the Manager of Plant Engineering, told me I should apply for a Senior Project Manager position. I knew I didn't have the qualifications to hold the position permanently, but once more, I was assigned on a temporary basis, until they found someone better. Or at least with more degrees. Still, I was glad for the opportunity to prove myself, and I always learnt a lot from taking on these added responsibilities.

What I didn't know was that Alex had a trick up his sleeve that made this time entirely different; he had sent an application for me to join the Society of Manufacturing Engineers, based on my knowledge and years of experience. He waited until the application was approved to tell me about it, and I was shocked beyond words. It was all I could do not to burst into tears right there in my supervisor's office.

Being a Senior Manufacturing Engineer gave me the qualifications to officially be hired on a permanent basis in senior management positions. It was a significant achievement I never believed I would attain, considering my very limited formal education.

It was just a piece of paper when you got down to it, but I was so proud to join such a prestigious society. I was now allowed to legally sign documents as an engineer without needing someone else to sign off on them.

Still, I wasn't complacent in my position, or my studies. I continued to take every course and seminar from the society of manufacturing engineers that I could manage, to improve my knowledge, and for future promotions.

These courses came in handy when I was later chosen to train the Corrective Action Team Leaders. As part of the Quality

Plus Process, they were tasked to improve the response time, so we could correct deficiencies throughout our organization. It all worked out very well, and I was asked to write a few articles about the process, which were published in the Pratt & Whitney Internal News Bulletin. Alex even requested that I go with him to Halifax, Nova Scotia, as a consultant, to select qualified General Contractors to implement the construction of a new manufacturing plant. It was quite an honor.

26

"O Lord, grant me the serenity to accept the things I cannot change. The courage to change the things I can, and the wisdom to know the difference."
-Reinhold Niebuhr

Although things were looking up at work, moving to the campground meant that I no longer had anywhere to just relax and not stress. I went to work, where I loved the added prestige and responsibilities, but it could get stressful. Then I went home to a slew of new problems I had to take care of at the campground. My work life was hectic, not to mention the financial burden of running a business.

On the family front, in addition to running the snack bar at the campground, Linda graduated from Concordia University with a Bachelor of Arts, majoring in Economics. I was incredibly proud of her accomplishment, as she was the first Wyngaert to graduate university; a feat that wouldn't be repeated for quite some time. Sandra was doing well, working in the accounting department at Pratt, and dating a boy from Verdun named Jean-Paul Petrin. Danny, on the other hand, had many issues to deal with because of choices he had made. A lot of teenagers lose their way, and Danny had fallen into the wrong crowd, getting involved in drugs and other bad habits, that I just didn't know how to help him out of.

The stress of everything put together was becoming unmanageable, as so many of the problems were out of my control. If you've been paying attention, you know that my solution to problems like this is usually to ignore them and keep working until something forces me to stop. This time, it was a heart attack. Or at least the symptoms of one, that brought me to the intensive care unit in July 1986.

My time in the hospital, as well as the months leading up to it, were a very dark period of my life. It got so bad that I seriously contemplated taking my own life. I was worn out and exhausted, and I couldn't see anything but continuous problems in my future, with no end in sight.

One of the planners in my department, Jean-Claude Poulin, came to visit me. He was one of the tradesmen who had helped me with the construction of my residence, and he recognized the signs of my depression, long before I owned up to them. He gave me a book by Og Mandino called The Greatest Miracle in the World, and told me it had helped him a lot when he was in a similar situation.

When the doctors finally discharged me, they put me on hypertension medication and told me I either had to change my life, or I would die. They might have been more delicate about it, but that was the general idea.

While I was recuperating, I read the book Jean-Claude gave me, then some other books by Mr. Mandino, also finding solace in the Serenity Prayer.

I was wasting so much stress on things I couldn't control, while ignoring the things that I could. I was in such a low point when I started reading them, but these books saved my life, giving me the hope that I could carry on. They changed my outlook on life, and helped me to make better choices in difficult situations, and with my life in general. They inspired me to be a better person.

I learnt not to pray for money, love, good health, fame, success, or happiness. You should pray for guidance, that you may be shown the way to acquire these things, and that is how your prayers will be answered.

I took all of this self-help and inspirational knowledge and wrote out letters to all of my nieces and nephews, sharing what I had learnt. I warned them to stay away from drugs, not from a place of preaching at them, but from a place of understanding. I told them what I had recently discovered, that the adversities they were experiencing would pass, and if they found a way through them instead of being overcome by them, they would be able to look back and laugh. I signed off with 'May God Bless You and Guide You'.

I also started writing letters to my family on their birthdays, instead of just giving them cards. Each letter would share all the milestones and adventures they had throughout the year, and be filled with what I hoped was wisdom and inspiration. Every time, I put 'May God Bless You and Guide You' at the bottom, with quotes to help them lead better lives. I sometimes worry they think it is silly, but they always seem to appreciate them. I have also been told by some of my nephews that they still have their letters to this day, and that they really helped them when they were going through hard times. If that is true for even one of them, then I did my job.

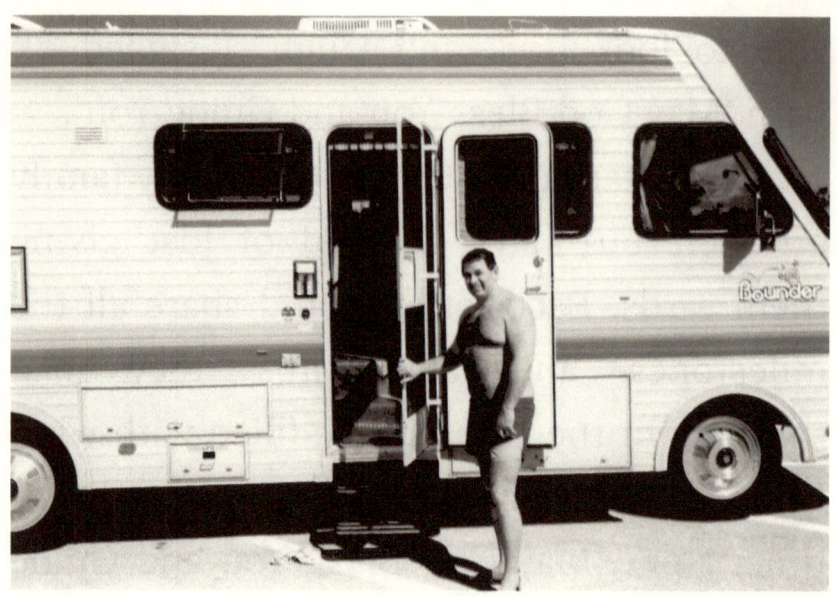

I took the doctor's advice to change my lifestyle and take more vacations by purchasing my first motorhome, a 31-foot Bounder. It was 65 000$, but the freedom and getaways it provided were priceless. I began to take time out for myself, and to focus on my mental health, which I had always glossed over in the past. In addition to the works of Og Mandino, I fed my mind with Napoleon Hill's Think and Grow Rich, Dale Carnegie's How to Win Friends and Influence People, Denis Waitley's Seeds of

Greatness, and especially Norman Vincent Peale's The Power of Positive Thinking. It truly encouraged me to be optimistic and grateful for what I had, because it could always be worse. I believe that these great authors played a big part in my success from that point on, and I thank them for the challenging and exciting life I continue to lead.

As for my son, he went through many rough patches, got lost and hit rock bottom, but then he found himself and turned his life around by going to rehab. He picked up many skills that other people his age never had the opportunity to, and capitalized on all of the experience he gained from working with me at the campground. Like me, he was never particularly good in school, so as my father did with me, I had him doing all of the manual work around the campground. He found his calling and was in his glory, doing anything mechanical, electrical, plumbing, or simply operating heavy equipment. He excelled.

Danny is probably one of the main reasons I continued to invest all the profits from the campground back into the business. We purchased a tractor, a golf cart, replaced electrical lines, and paved the main road. I obviously wanted to provide better facilities for my campers and more revenues for myself, but I needed to secure this stable career for my son.

With Danny taking care of the grounds, and the girls in the office, Barb and I were able to begin our new lifestyle of travelling frequently, especially once the camping season was over. We went on many summer getaways, then escaped to warmer destinations in the colder months. We planned to continue to travel like that for the rest of our lives.

27

*"One day your life will flash before your eyes.
Make sure it's worth watching."*
-Anonymous

In the spring of 1987, Barbara and I got the shock of our lives when we found out that she was pregnant. None of our children were planned, they were all happy accidents, but this was something altogether different. Our oldest child was married and our youngest was twenty-two!

Barbara had an aunt who was born to a mother of a certain age, and had the mental capacity of a seven year old as a result. Barb did not want to risk the same thing happening, but I was a catholic, and couldn't let her do differently.

We told the kids, who found it absolutely hilarious. One day we were at the dinner table, enjoying a meal together, when they all took out baby rattles to tease us. They thought they were pretty clever, but we weren't laughing.

At the time, Linda was working for a radio station, attempting to secure advertisements, and she hated it. Nearly every morning on her way to work, she would have to pull over onto the side of the road so she could throw up. We wondered if she could be pregnant, but she insisted it was because she hated her job so much that it was making her sick.

Before long, Barbara miscarried, which at this point in her life, she saw as a relief. Almost immediately after, we found out that Linda was expecting our first grandchild, which made a lot more sense.

SINCE BARB and I needed to travel for my health, Linda gave up the snack bar, so Bobby could run it with his sister, Carol, and Linda could man the office with Sandra while we went away. It was around this time that the Government told us we had to immediately stop the Paintball Games in the Woods. Apparently, it didn't comply with the zoning of the land, which we later found out was code for 'the Vallée du Richelieu Golf Club is worried the golfers will be disturbed by what happens in the woods half a mile away'. The

Paintball Games had been a lifesaver in the early days when we had no campers, but things had gradually started to pick up, and we no longer needed them to drum up business. It was sad for our campers, and the snack bar, but not as devastating as it would have been years before.

Me, Roger, Kay, Kenny, Al, Phil, Louise, Diane, and Barbara.

On the first weekend in June, Barb and I took our motorhome to Plattsburgh, where we met up with Roger, Kay, Georges and Denise. It was a lovely weekend trip, but there was a lake there with green water. The color wasn't so bad, but the broken beer bottles and pollution ensured that no one wanted to go swimming. Except for me. I can't say if it was because I was so eager to enjoy the summer, or if I was trying to show that it would take more than a bit of garbage to scare me, but I do remember that Barb made me shower before she would let me kiss her.

LATER ON THAT WEEK, when we were back home, my right leg took on this reddish color that Barb described as 'raw meat'. So, on June 11th, I went to Pierre Boucher Hospital and was diagnosed with cellulitis erysipelas-streptococcus group A, an infection similar to flesh-eating disease. They treated me with a very strong antibiotic, both intravenously and in pill form, for six days.

While I was in the hospital, I read a lot of self-help books and ones on positive thinking, but when my course of antibiotics was done, my leg looked the same. They concluded their treatment wasn't effective.

Their fear was that it would spread, so if they weren't able to get rid of it, they were going to have to amputate my leg. I could not let this happen. I read up and did my own research, discovering an article on tick bites. Apparently, they caused similar problems and could be very difficult to diagnose, as most doctors wouldn't consider it unless they saw a bite. I knew that I had been swimming in polluted waters, so I was relieved I figured it out.

I told my doctors, expecting them to give me the proper treatment so I could go home, legs intact, but they did not listen. They kept me on a course of treatment that was wasting precious time, wasn't working, and might be doing me more damage than good. I was not pleased.

As they had no intentions of changing the medication they were treating me with, I checked myself out of the hospital, against medical advice. I set out to find a doctor who would prescribe me a more effective drug to treat my disease, that I believed to be a tick bite, but it was no use. I went to three different doctors, and each one insisted I continue with the original antibiotic that wasn't working.

Every day, my leg got worse. I was desperate to find a doctor who would prescribe me another drug, even if it wasn't the one I suggested, just to try something different that might actually work.

On July 13th, I went back to my first doctor, Dr. Jean-Marie Martel, and begged him to look at the article I had read, showing him that it was from a medical journal. He was reluctant, but finally agreed to give me a prescription for a drug called Duricep, which they usually used to treat skin infections like Lyme disease.

By the time I went to my follow up appointment with Dr. Martel, I had made an unbelievable recovery. He could not believe how much I had improved. My energy was returning, and the raw meat look of my right leg had disappeared. He told me it was the first time in his professional career that a patient successfully recommended his own medication. If he is still practicing today, I am sure it wasn't his last.

I WANT to take a moment to say that in my life, I have been faced with the most incompetent doctors imaginable, but graced with the most incredible ones as well. A lot of patients go to doctors with crazy theories about what is wrong with them, so I understand not listening to every suggestion a patient makes. But I owe my leg, and possibly my life, to the fact that one doctor finally agreed to look outside the box and try something different. It took a hell of a lot of convincing. Someone less confident, or more polite, would have let the doctors cut off their leg. It is imperative that you advocate for yourself, because most of the time, no one else will.

It was a slow and gradual journey to regain my health by exercising daily and body building with weights. It was a miracle that my leg was not amputated, but I think the huge quantities of the wrong antibiotic may have created problems with my immune system for years to come. Either way, I needed to get my body into top shape for my granddaughter.

Chelsea Rachel Cavanagh was born on November 30th 1987, making me the happiest man on earth. She was the greatest gift I ever could have wished for; perfect in every way. This miracle of life was the beginning of a new generation in our family, giving me a completely new outlook on life. Like her mother's birth years before, Chelsea's gave us a new purpose. We wanted nothing more than to experience the joy of our first grandchild growing up, and to witness all of her great achievements. We knew, even then, that there would be many.

28

"The difference between who I am and who I want to be is only separated by what I do."
-Unknown

My doctor recommended I find a way to lose weight to help control my blood pressure, so I joined Weight Watchers in 1988. Linda, Barb's sister Carole, and Danny's girlfriend Lynn joined as well. Lynn was the daughter of Mike Blanchard, who worked with me back in my bouncer days, and the kids all grew up together, so we were absolutely thrilled that she and Danny were dating. Barb and Sandra were already lifetime members of Weight Watchers, so we had a lot of support, and the added motivation of Sandra's upcoming wedding. Not to mention, Sandra would practically pull food out of our mouths if we tried to overindulge. My health continued to improve as I lost more and more weight. I never made it to my goal, but I got to 199 lbs, which was the lowest I had been in a while.

Me, Sandra, JP, and Barbara.

Sandra married JP Petrin on April 30th 1988, with a reception at Hélène de Champlain. Contrary to the conventions of the time, Sandra had both Barbara and I give her away. I had never seen this done before, but Sandra felt that we both raised her, and both deserved to be up there with her. At the time, I had my doubts about JP, but over the years he has proven to be a reliable and thoughtful son-in-law, who is always ready to lend a hand and will bend over backwards to help us out.

AT PRATT, I was promoted to a higher grade of Senior Project Manager in recognition for my extraordinary effectiveness and value control proposals, which saved Pratt hundreds of thousands of dollars. I was on cloud nine.

To help improve my public speaking abilities, I joined the Teleglobe Toastmasters International Club. It was a great asset for me, as more and more of my new assignments required expressing myself in groups of people. Sometimes rather large ones, such as when I was sent to represent Pratt & Whitney Canada instead of my supervisor, at a conference for managers from all divisions of United Technologies.

It was held in Hartford, Connecticut, and I was probably the only person in the group of sixty or so representatives who didn't have an engineering degree, or better. Due to time restraints, they randomly selected six managers to go on stage and report the cost of maintaining the facilities that came under their responsibility. As luck would have it, I was chosen to go first. Although I was well prepared and had all of my figures, there is no way I could have pulled it off without those public speaking courses.

In September, we took a trip out to Lac Labelle, where Danny and Lynn owned a cottage. Linda and Cazzie also came, bringing little Chelsea, who made every occasion brighter and more fun. The only way you could reach their cabin, which was on an island without electricity, was by boat, then up a wooden staircase on a hillside.

As the sun was setting and we called it a day, I was the one holding Chelsea to go back to the boat. They were still renovating, so there was no railing around the balcony to show you where the staircase was. Although it was dark by then, I was confident I was stepping in the right place, until I fell into the void. It was like the world around me stopped as I tried to protect Chelsea in my arms, hearing my daughter scream in a way you never want to hear a mother scream.

I rolled down the hill for what felt like forever, but it was also over in an instant. I immediately got up and checked on Chelsea, who was crying fiercely. We brought her to the hospital as fast as we could, given our location, and concluded that she had been crying from the shock. There wasn't even a scratch on her!

I, on the other hand, was a complete mess. I paid for it in the days to come, but I would have given my life many times over to protect that little girl.

29

"Don't back down just to keep the peace. Standing up for your beliefs builds self-confidence and self-esteem."
-Oprah Winfrey

At Pratt, I was assigned to a major project; the dehumidification of plant #1. It had a factory floor of approximately one million square feet, but every time the temperature reached 90 degrees Fahrenheit, everyone inside had to stop working until it went back to safer levels. This resulted in millions of dollars in lost production hours, every year. They were happy to spend 15 million dollars to fix it once and for all.

I attended my first meeting to plan, direct, and implement the project with the chief of our mechanical engineering department, Guy Jobidon, and the consultant group, Pageau Morel. They had already been working on their design for many months, but when I looked at the drawing and specifications, I saw a lot of opportunities to make it better, or at least more cost effective.

I have noticed that even if a task could take fifteen minutes to do, if you give someone an hour to complete it, most people will take the whole hour. The same goes for money. If you give them a certain budget to accomplish something, most people will use it. I don't know if it is because I grew up fighting for every penny, or because I owned apartment buildings, a restaurant and a campground with next to no budget, but I always asked myself: How can I do this better? How can I be more efficient? How can this cost less money?

FOR INSTANCE, United Aircraft Technologies had a program called Value Control Proposals, where all employees were invited to submit cost-saving or problem-solving ideas. If the company thought your idea had merit, or if they implemented it, you would receive an award, which sometimes translated to a cash prize. The first time I won, we bought the family a St-Bernard dog we called Brutus. The kids weren't the best at taking care of him, and I didn't want Barb to be saddled with all of the responsibilities, so I found a way to automate some of them. I made Brutus a special trough, with a valve that linked to our water line, so he got fresh water simply by pressing his tongue down on the plate. I also put Brutus' leash on a steel clothesline, so he could wander the yard freely, and we wouldn't have to walk him as often. I worked hard, but I also worked smart.

ROBERT WYNGAERT

This was posted around Pratt & Whitney around this time.

I requested major changes, but my coworkers were not pleased by my initiative, and refused to change anything. I wrote a letter to Alex and explained to him that I couldn't manage the project the way it was designed. He told me this was insubordination and grounds for dismissal.

I probably should have shut my mouth then and played nice, now that I had voiced my reluctance. However, my word and my reputation were all I had, and I couldn't put them at stake for a project I didn't think would succeed. So, I wrote another letter, this time outlining my plan, and how it would save them millions of dollars. I staked my reputation and my livelihood on it, saying they could fire me if I was wrong, and implement their original design. Alex told me I was the most tenacious guy he'd ever met.

He discussed it with Royal, still the director of Plant Engineering, and the two of them tried, to no avail, to convince Mr. Jobidon to consider my proposal. According to him, his project had been approved by a top-rated consultant firm, so if any changes were made, his entire department would refuse to support us. This put Alex in a very difficult situation.

Luckily, Alex was a very intelligent man who had a lot of confidence in me, so he set up a meeting with the consultants, engineers, and president of Pageau Morel so they could review my proposal compared to theirs.

The president, Mr. Lefebvre brought me to fancy, expensive restaurants for our meetings, probably to convince me to accept their plans, but I held my ground. I believe Mr. Lefebvre was an educated man, who saw the benefits and value in my proposal, but couldn't let his team down, so he asked me to approve the original plans. I told him I would rather be fired on the spot than to approve their design. He got up, gave me a firm handshake and said he had rarely met a person like me.

I didn't know I had won him over until I arrived in our next meeting and saw that the drawings, specifications, and budget had been revised to implement my proposed design. I had to take full responsibility for the project, and accomplish it without the support of the mechanical plant engineering department, as Mr. Jobidon still didn't agree with my revisions. It was a lot of pressure, but I felt confident in the proposal, and was anxious to prove Mr. Jobidon wrong.

The dehumidification project took about a year to complete, from conception to implementation. As our deadline got closer and closer, my stress levels went higher and higher, until I had a heart attack on May 1st 1990, the day we were supposed to put our new system to work. I was rushed to the Montreal General Hospital and underwent a coronary angioplasty to unblock my right artery. I spent twelve days in an intensive care unit, which was very stressful for everyone.

It was while I was in the hospital that I was told the system didn't function as planned when they launched it. On the day I was released from the hospital, my family wanted me to come home and keep resting, but I insisted on dropping by the plant so I could see what went wrong.

After reviewing the start-up plan of action, I noticed that the old ventilation and air systems were not disabled, as I had requested. I personally escorted one of our maintenance electricians to all the penthouses to ensure the old systems were put out of commission. They weren't needed with the new dehumidification system, so I had the fuses removed and the wires cut.

We restarted my new system and it functioned perfectly. It was quite a relief, but an even greater accomplishment. My plan saved the company millions of dollars, on a project that would save the company millions of dollars every year by completely eliminating the downtime.

After the new system had been running for a few weeks, the President, Dave Caplan, invited me to his office to thank me for implementing such a difficult project without even stopping production. He couldn't believe the results.

He brought me out onto the floor and said, "I believe the shop is more comfortable than my office!"

This entire process was a big advantage for my career as senior project manager, and gained me the respect of my supervisors, peers, consultants and subordinates. Even Mr. Jobidon!

It was one of the most significant events of my life. I want to say the respect meant more to me than the salary increase, but I don't want to lie, so I'll say it was a very close second at the time.

Now though, it is entirely the respect I earned and the pride I felt in the accomplishment that I remember.

30

"What we call failure is not the falling down but the staying down."
-Mary Pickford

Lynn, Danny, Barbara, Me, Ethel and Mike Blanchard.

Danny and Lynn got married on September 9th, 1989. Our kids didn't live together after their weddings like I did with Georges, but it made me really happy to see how close everyone was, especially the girls. Lynn had started working for us at the campground, so having the three of them working together all summer made them more like sisters than sisters-in-law. I was so happy to see all of my children happy and settled in their new lives.

. . .

On April 11TH 1990, Sandra gave birth to a baby girl, Amanda Lynn Petrin, in the middle of a snowstorm. She was another bright spot in our lives, that helped me forget the stress of the dehumidification project. Barbara and I were thrilled to have two granddaughters to spoil!

After the completion of my first dehumidification project, I was assigned to another one, this time for Plant #5. They involved me from the very beginning, allowing me to contribute to the conception, as well as the implementation. I also got to define the plans to do the same in the warehouse of Plant #1. Their goal was always to eliminate down time, but mine was to complete the projects on time and under budget. I succeeded every time.

I no longer had to worry about proving my competence or working harder and longer to feel like I earned my salary. I had often experienced my own imposter syndrome, being the only non-engineer in the room, but I now felt like I belonged. We were all there to improve the efficiency of the company, so it could remain competitive in the market and earn world recognition for their gas turbine engines, and I was doing my part.

Building our retirement home.

In planning for our retirement, Barb and I purchased 1.2 acres of lakefront land in Rouses Point, New York. It was the perfect spot, close enough to home that we would never be far from the family, but far enough away that the campground problems couldn't get to us, with beautiful Lake Champlain in our backyard. The land cost $47,000, and we hired a local General Contractor to build our dream retirement residence for $100 000.

Due to my experience dealing with contractors and writing specifications, I made everything very clear for him, including the delivery dates. However, I do not believe that his team understood any of my schedules or specifications. They were nothing like the tradesmen I was used to dealing with back home.

When I saw that they were never going to deliver what I wanted, I cancelled the contract. I still paid $100 000 for the man-hours and materials he claimed I owed him for, because I did not want to have any problems with him. It was frustrating to pay for a finished job when it was barely halfway done.

Once his team was out, I took over, not used to projects being off-schedule, over-budget, and with poor workmanship. I relied on old friends and family to help me finish the project. I am so grateful to Marco Bissonnette, Raymond Huard, Bobby and Moe, as well as my family, who were all instrumental in the building of our new home.

31

"At the end of life, what really matters is not what we bought, but what we built; not what we got, but what we shared; not our competence, but our character; and not our success, but our significance. Live a life that matters. Live a life of love."
-Unknown

I got three new grandbabies in 1991. Rikki Christine Cavanagh was born on

March 31st, Steven Michel Wyngaert on July 16th, and Paul Ryan Petrin on October 30th. It was so wonderful to have them born so close together, discovering milestones and growing with each other. Since Sandra didn't go back to work after Amanda, she ran a family day care service. The five of them were biologically cousins, but they were much more like siblings. Watching them together was my greatest joy, as family is everything.

UNBELIEVABLE BUT TRUE

Rikki, Amanda, Paul, Chelsea, and Steve.

The campground was getting busier every year, but winters were pretty quiet, so Danny tried his hand at a woodcutting business. I let him cut the trees on our lands, destroying roughly fifteen acres for absolutely no profit. It was a failure, financially and as a business venture, but it was also a source of pride for me to see my son working so hard to accomplish something. I was finally beginning to see a return on my latest investment of the campground, but I went through a lot of failures and bad investments before I got there. It was nice to see my son taking on the same path, although I knew from experience it could be a long and very hard one.

AT PRATT, I was doing so well that they routinely assigned me the most difficult projects that other people didn't want to take. I was very touched by the confidence they had in me, but I sometimes wished I could just relax with one of the smaller, easier projects that didn't involve so much pressure.

My current project was a ten-million-dollar expansion of Plant #5 for a new cleaning, plating, and waste treatment facility which should be completed by January 1993.

I completed the dehumidification of Plant #5 and wrote an article in the Pratt news bulletin about it. We finished within our four-million-dollar budget, and on schedule, thanks to my three-shift system of working on it seven days a week. Start to finish, it only took ten weeks, meaning we were done before the heat of the summer months could cost the company millions in mandatory work stoppages.

32

"You are never too old to set another goal or to dream a new dream."
-C.S. Lewis

In 1993, I started my year off with a few trips to the hospital, though thankfully they were both planned. On January 28th, I had surgery on my knee, then on February 3rd, I got lasik surgery on my eyes. I am a strong proponent of investing in yourself, which comes in many shapes and sizes. For me it mostly meant investing in courses and my education, as I was constantly trying to make up for the fact that I never made it to high school when I was a child. As I got older, it meant investing in my retirement fund, and ensuring that Barb and I would be taken care of. Now, I was investing in my physical health and fitness, so I could continue doing the things I needed to do without being encumbered.

Many years later, when my niece, Melanie, wanted to get that same lasik surgery, she came to me and asked for a loan. I saw that she was investing in herself, both in her health and in her confidence, so I decided to help her out. I lent her the money, but instead of having her pay me back with interest, I had her invest it with my daughter, Linda. My niece opened an account and started to send money into it every month, thinking it would go towards paying me back. After a year or so, she had saved the amount that I lent her, but instead of taking it back, I let it be the start of her investing in her own future. The initial amount may not have been that much, but she continued to send money into that account, as faithfully as if it were a bill, and was eventually able to buy herself a condo because of it.

My last project at Pratt was the expansion of Plant #5. Once more, I completed it on time and within budget, my reputation intact as I took an early retirement. Or at least I retired from Pratt, as I was going to be working as an independent businessman at the campground full time. And hopefully spending lots of time with my family.

My last day with Pratt & Whitney was,

quite fittingly, March 30th – my fifty-fifth birthday.

Mr. Abedda, one of my employees who painted the portrait of me you see in the background.

On April 2nd, my retirement party was held at Kenny Wong's restaurant. I had been to a few of these before, so I was expecting a dozen, maybe twenty-five people would come, we would have a delicious meal, then Barb and I would go home and get into the routine of running our campground.

Instead, I showed up and found 126 of my supervisors, peers, subordinates, consultants, tradesmen, and family members. Barb was there with the kids and their significant others, Georges came with Irene, Marilyne with Manfred, Bobby with Moe, Kenny with Louise…they all came to support me! I was shocked, not just that so many people had been invited, but that most of them had shown up, even with the terrible snow storm we had that day.

I could never find the words to tell all the people in that room how much I appreciated their participation in such a wonderful celebration. I wish I could thank every single person who contributed to my success at Pratt & Whitney, both big and small.

Nicole Comeau and Muriel Leger, who did most of the work to organize the party, did a fabulous job, and really went the extra mile to make everything perfect, from the guest list to the decorations, the venue and the food. They even hired a professional photographer and assembled a photo album that they gave me several weeks after the event.

It seemed like everyone was sad to see me go, but wished me continued success in my future endeavors. All of the speakers had praise and compliments for me regarding my career, except for Mr. Leger, who told a story he found funny, but I did not. Apparently, he had asked Barbara what my best quality was, and she said I was a great provider. When he said everyone provides and that answer doesn't count, Barb supposedly said I had a quick temper. Which isn't a quality at all. I was not pleased, but everyone there laughed.

In addition to the photo album, I was presented with priceless gifts on the night of the party. There was a hand-painted portrait of me, a wood sculpture, a Brass eagle (Pratt's trademark), a painting of Plant #5 (the last project I managed), and a beautiful Canon Camera.

SOMEONE WHO DIDN'T KNOW me might have assumed that this would be my easiest summer yet, since I wouldn't have to juggle multiple jobs, but it was anything but. I finally had the time and energy to devote myself fully to the campground, making plans and implementing all of the ideas I had to make it better. Every year so far had been better than the last, but this year we broke records, increasing our revenues by 10%!

Some people commented on how lucky I was to have such a successful enterprise, but I told them, 'the harder I work, the luckier I get'. Being at the campground day in and day out also allowed me to see just how true it is that you can't succeed on your own. I never could have accomplished my dreams without the help of my beautiful wife, and my wonderful children, who not only supported me in my pursuit, but worked hard every day to make it a reality. They deserve a large chunk of the credit.

IN THE FALL, I received a call from Jacques Bissonnette, the president of Soprin Consultant Firm. He heard that I retired, and after all of our dealings together, both at Pratt and with his firm for the restaurant, he was wondering if I would like to work with him.

It was an incredible offer. Before retiring, I wouldn't have dreamed of saying no to him, but I had big plans for the campground now. We were in the process of making a new storage area, where the spots would each have a number, and it would be fenced in for extra security. Jacques told me the project he was thinking of me for was to manage the construction of aircraft engine test cells at the Rolls Royce Facilities in Montreal, which sounded like a dream come true.

I was leaving for Cape Coral, to visit Roger, so I told him I would make my decision and call him back upon my return. As it turns out, we got back from Florida just in time for the birth of our sixth and final grandchild. Eric Robert Wyngaert was born to Danny and Lynn on November 17th, 1993.

The creation of life has always given me a high, as I believe that family is the most important thing. I analyzed the pros and cons of Jacques' offer, and ultimately decided to refuse it. From a business standpoint, I was in the process of making a large investment in my campground, and I wanted to see it through. I wanted to bring Camping Alouette to another level by achieving a five-star rating across the board.

More importantly, I could see that I was building a family unlike any I had experienced before. I saw all three of my children, and all six of my grandchildren, on an almost daily basis. I was experiencing all of the milestones and moments that I was too busy working to experience with my own children. This was my second chance to be a part of their lives and to watch them grow up, and I didn't want to miss it.

Luckily, I thought of a mechanical engineer I had worked with before, who was more than qualified, and would definitely be interested.

IV

RETIREMENT

33

"The purpose of life is to live it, to taste experience to the utmost, to reach out eagerly and without fear for newer and richer experience."
-Eleanor Roosevelt

Barb and I finally became financially independent in 1994. In May, we sold our retirement lakehouse in New York for $200 000 and bought a 38-foot Friendship motorhome instead. The people who bought our house weren't able to secure a mortgage, so they gave me a $50 000 down payment, and monthly payments for the next few years. It was a nice surprise every time the U.S. dollar went up!

The sale not only brought in money, it also saved us all of the insurance and utilities that we had to pay year-round, whether we were at the house or not. Combined with my package from Pratt, and the campground's record year, this meant that we had the equity – or borrowing power – to invest in large projects.

After enduring a lifetime of stress and struggles, career challenges and financial crises, I finally felt like we had made it.

. . .

MOST OF MY work at the campground was getting everything ready in the spring, and closing it down in the fall. Now that we had a motorhome, we spent every weekend of the summer exploring Magog, Ottawa, Quebec City...anywhere that was a few hours away from home. Barb and I made it to every State and Province in North America, with the exception of Newfoundland and Alaska. Georges and Denise often came with us in their motorhome, or we would meet up with friends or family members, depending on the destination. I felt like Barb and I deserved these mini vacations, but we were also assessing our competitors. Every campground we went to gave us ideas for how we could invest our resources to better serve our clientele, which was one of my top priorities.

. . .

WORKING for Pratt had taught me how to forecast and propose expenditures, but it also taught me that the person in charge isn't always the one with the best ideas. That is why I insisted on having Round Robin meetings at the beginning and end of every season, to get everyone's input. I would determine how much funds we had at our disposal, then we would all discuss what we wanted to spend them on. We would determine what was important, then prioritize what needed to be done immediately, making five-year plans to ensure growth.

I knew it was important that everyone felt pride in their work, and that they had a say in what was going on. In 1994, our funds went to creating more sites - thirteen of them pull-throughs, renovating the washrooms and main building, a new tractor, and trying to improve our drainage; a task that would resurface every time it rained. Other years we purchased land, army trucks, materials, anything that would help us develop more sites and accommodate our growing bank of customers.

One of our best investments was creating storage spots. We purchased 100 000 square feet of commercial land behind our neighbor, VR Dumont Inc., when they went bankrupt. It was right next to our existing storage area, so we expanded it to meet the growing demand for RV storage. It cost $75 000 to develop the land, but we got an additional forty storage spaces, which brought a return on investment within four years.

34

"You are the master of your destiny. You can influence, direct and control your own environment. You can make your life what you want it to be."
– Napoleon Hill

In 1995, we did something different for our winter vacation. On January 14th, we set off in the motorhome on the longest trip of our lives. Sandra's family had recently moved to Ontario, so our first stop was a karaoke party at her house, with some of Barb's siblings joining in. We then went through Missouri, Tennessee, Oklahoma, and Texas before arriving in Las Vegas, Nevada. Barb and I had never been, so we enjoyed the casinos and the many free shows offered by the hotels.

I believe it was at MGM that I paid to have my picture taken and placed on an Adventure Magazine cover. They put my face over Indiana Jones' body, so it looked like I had been having adventures in the jungle. I may have played into this, so for the next decade, my grandchildren believed that I went on a safari and wrestled with alligators, lifted hippopotamuses, and became Tarzan. I never told them it wasn't true, so it took them watching the Indiana Jones movies as teenagers to put it together. I was sad to be discovered, but I enjoyed many years of my grandchildren arguing,

ROBERT WYNGAERT

"My grandfather's stronger than your dad" whenever the argument came up.

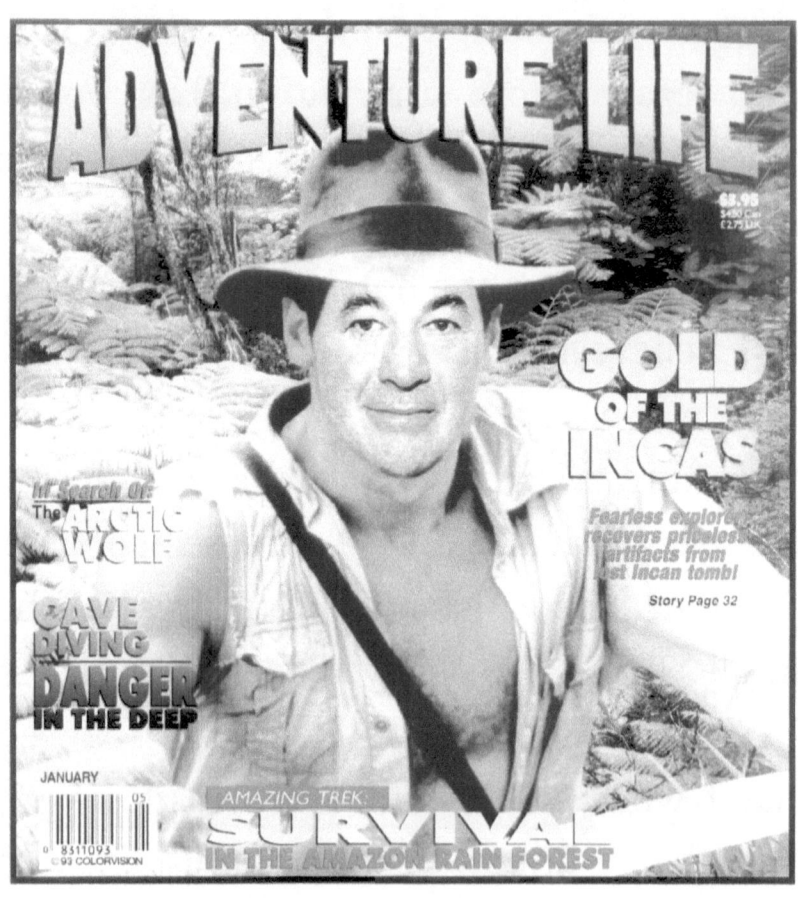

AFTER VEGAS, we spent some time in Cape Coral visiting Roger before we came home after forty-three days and over thirteen thousand kilometers. It was a fantastic experience, but we were happy to be home. I would never have imagined taking such an extended vacation, but after my doctor told me I had to change my lifestyle, I was determined to take him seriously. I was definitely enjoying life more, but that included a lot of delicious food, which was something I might need to work on. It definitely made a difference to be travelling so often, and spending all of my other meals in the very capable hands of my favorite chef, my beautiful Barb.

IN ADDITION TO VACATIONS, I also implemented all of the improvements we planned for the campground, most of them based on our travels. I always made it a point to reinvest the net profits back into the business, so we could provide the best facilities in the most economical manner.

Thanks to all of my years at Pratt, and previous construction experience with my dad, I was usually able to get by with just myself, Danny, and our employees. This gave us substantial savings, and allowed our investments to go so much further than Ken and Dan could ever have imagined back when they owned it. We were quickly becoming a top-rated campground, building a reputation others in the industry strived to achieve, but we didn't want to become complacent with our success. I believe it is this drive I had, to compete with every campground I met on my travels, that was instrumental in improving campground facilities and utility services throughout the entire province of Quebec.

It usually came to an average of one hundred-thousand dollars per year in managed and capital expenditures, such as developing new pull-through sites, asphalting the roads, refurbishing the game room and playground, updating our maintenance equipment, motor vehicles and tractors, etc.

35

"A positive thinker does not refuse to recognize the negative; he refuses to dwell on it. Positive thinking is a form of thought which habitually looks for the best results from the worst conditions."
- Norman Vincent Peale

On January 16th 1996, I started having chest pains, so Barbara drove me to the Charles Lemoyne Hospital. They admitted me for observation as soon as I arrived, and reproached us for not calling an ambulance instead. Barb was not happy, as I was the one who had insisted on her driving me. Part of it was me absolutely not wanting to be brought to Pierre Boucher hospital, which was the closest, but I think I also thought that as long as I could arrive by car, it wasn't that serious.

I was in the hospital for four days and diagnosed with angina. This time it wasn't the stress of my busy life that got to me, it was my weight. I was at my highest ever, 245 pounds.

I started reading a book by Oprah and Bob Greene, the Journal of Daily Renewal, and managed to get down to 200 lbs by April. To celebrate, we traded in our Friendship motorhome for a brand-new Scenic Cruiser. It was quite the expense, but after all the hard work we'd put in over the years, we deserved it.

ROBERT WYNGAERT

On May 9th, I was driving our tractor down one of our hills, but it was going much too fast for my liking. I tried to press down harder on the brakes, but I realized that they weren't working at all. I didn't know if they were being difficult, or completely disconnected, and I didn't want to waste time trying to fix them as I gained speed. I knew the farther I went, the faster I would be going, and I didn't want to crash into anything of value, or – god forbid – anyone. So, I steered myself into a tree.

As you've probably come to expect from me, I got up and walked it off. That is, I walked from my crash site back to the main office and tried to go on with my day, but I was in a lot of pain. It turned out that I fractured a rib.

There was still a lot of work to be done to prepare for the camping season, so JP moved back from Ontario a few months early to help Danny get everything ready. It wasn't like I sat around and did nothing, but I did have to keep a slower pace for almost a month after the accident, before I could go back to my usual routine.

SINCE SANDRA WAS MOVING HOME, Linda began a new career as a Certified Financial Advisor, letting Sandra take over as General Manager of Camping Alouette. If only Linda had started this career earlier, I would have avoided many blunders, and been much richer!

For example, in 1999, Linda convinced me to multiply our capital gains exemption by giving each of my children shares of the corporation through an Estate Freeze and a Family Trust. When I brought it up with my accountant, he told me that was something very wealthy people would do, but not a small business owner like me. Still, I imagined that it would be useful for the kids when Barb and I died. I have always trusted my daughter implicitly.

36

"A candle loses nothing by lighting another candle."
-James Keller

I believe that it is not easy to be successful. It requires a strong will and perseverance, because quality is never an accident. It is the result of high intentions, sincere effort, intelligent direction, and skillful execution. It represents the wise choice out of many alternatives. Throughout my career, my businesses, and my family life, I have always tried to make the right choices.

That is why it was so hard for me when the Federal government came to audit my business and personal finances. I can deal with deadlines and multi-million dollar projects, but this was the most stressful experience I had ever been through. After working countless hours and multiple jobs for forty years, they were combing through my receipts, saying I owed for unpaid income taxes on the business.

The auditors investigated every business and personal expenditure, inquiring about our credit cards, bank accounts, telephone records…they left no stone unturned. Everything was fair game, including where we went on vacation and how much we spent on each trip. They were ruthless. Luckily, I have always kept meticulous records of my projects and expenditures, and I had taken note of all of the contests I won at Pratt to pay for most of our trips, but none of it seemed to be enough for the auditors.

Eventually, they stopped asking for things, so we assumed they were satisfied and everything was settled. We usually left for longer trips once the camping season was over, but given how stressed the audit made us, we left for a month-long trip in the middle of August! We went all the way to Vancouver, stopping in on old friends and family members along the way. We got to visit the Amish settlements in Indiana while having our motorhome repaired, marvelled at the glaciers and Lake Louise, then visited Mount Rushmore before coming home.

WHEN I HEARD that the Camping Canada convention, where campground owners get together for workshops and lectures on best practices in the industry, would be in Nashville, Tennessee, I immediately signed up for it, and planned another vacation around those dates. Barb and I left Sandra and Danny in charge of the campground and headed out in our motorhome.

We stayed at the KOA Opryland campground, hoping to catch a few country shows while we were there. We expected to meet a lot of campground owners, as it was a much bigger convention than the ones we usually attended, but we didn't think we would see any French Quebecers. Imagine our surprise when we ran into Normand Jacques, the president of Camping Quebec, and Maryse Catellier, the secretary.

We went for dinner together, where I had a fantastic 20 oz. porterhouse steak. I was very embarrassed when they wouldn't let me pay, but I promised I would make up for it.

On the first day of the conference, we attended the seminars with them. One of the most beneficial parts of these conventions is the conversation that happens during the breaks and meals. It is one thing to have a person tell you about an ideal, but it is quite another to share ideas with people who have real-world experience with the same problems you do.

The next day, we introduced Normand and Maryse to the vendors that supplied us with the campground utilities that are not available in Quebec, like electrical boxes. I could tell by the look on their faces that this was how I was paying them back for that supper they paid on the first night. It was a game-changer, not just for Normand and Maryse, but for all of Quebec. We were the only ones at the time who were importing the necessary utility boxes specially designed for campground hookups, but after our introductions, the Camping Quebec Association imported thousands of units and made them available to all of their owners. It brought the Quebec camping industry to a whole new level.

Robert Thompson at his eightieth birthday party.

Over Thanksgiving weekend in 1996, we hosted an eightieth birthday party for Barbara's father. Every year since he turned seventy-five, she insisted on throwing him a big party, arguing that it might be his last. We knew how lucky we were that he was still with us, watching his teenage great-grandchildren grow up, and we didn't want to take it for granted.

The family all got together in our old Arcade and we ordered BBQ chicken – nowhere near as good as the ones he used to make at our restaurant – and spent the day dancing, partying, and singing. He slept over, since his wife was in Rawdon for the weekend, then Barb and Ronnie drove him home.

UNFORTUNATELY, Barb's father had been having a lot of health issues, and within weeks he needed someone by his side 24/7. Even though we had the big parties every year in case this happened, none of us was anywhere near ready for it when he passed away that November. He had been a constant source of love, support and encouragement for everyone who knew him.

From the moment I started dating Barbara, he became a close friend, offering advice and stories to me for the past forty years. For the grandkids, this was the first person they knew who died, and it was probably the first time they saw me cry. His death left a huge hole in all of our lives.

C̲h̲r̲i̲s̲t̲m̲a̲s̲ ̲w̲a̲s̲ hard for all of the adults, but thankfully, the children were too young to understand the loss. They were a bright light in all of our dark worlds.

37

"*The tests of life are not to break you but to make you.*"
-Norman Vincent Peale

Chelsea, Steve, Amanda, Paul, Rikki, and Eric at Disney in 1997.

ROBERT WYNGAERT

When we returned from a family vacation to Walt Disney World in March of 1997, the Federal Government announced that they'd completed their audit of our revenues. As I was under the impression we had settled the matter a year earlier, I was quite shocked to find out they thought we owed $250 000 of unpaid income taxes. There was no way this was possible, but unfortunately, the burden was on me to prove them wrong. I thought the stress was going to eat me alive.

BARB WASN'T DOING SO WELL around this time either. Losing her father really took a toll on her. She spent two months with bronchitis, and the coughing didn't let up for months afterwards. She was also diagnosed with high blood pressure, so she was glad to be able to get back to her exercise program once the bronchitis cleared. Every morning, she would walk around the entire campground, marking off if any customers arrived during the night, left early, or had unregistered visitors. Nothing got past her!

This was all done before she made breakfast for me, and whoever was working in the store that day.

It took months of negotiations between Revenue Canada and my Chartered Accountant, Jean Pilotte, before I was able to prove them wrong. Upon review, we settled on $48 000 to close the case. I probably could have brought it down lower, because I truly did not owe that money, but the stress was more than I could take, and my health was worth more than that.

. . .

After all of the audit stress, we really needed another vacation, so Barbara and I headed for Myrtle Beach on September 5th. My brothers both came with us; Roger staying in a mobile home and Georges with his motorhome. We had excellent weather that made it a joy to walk along the beach and go swimming, for everyone except me. I was having chest pains and shortness of breath, so I couldn't keep up with the others.

True to form, I ignored my pain and tried to have a pleasant vacation. We went to watch Eddie Miles (the best Elvis impersonator I have ever seen), The Legends, Ripley's Believe it or Not, the Dixie Stampede, etc. We had a great time, but no matter how much I ignored them, my chest pains didn't go away.

. . .

AFTER MY BROTHERS and their wives went home, Barb told me I had to go to the hospital, to make sure I wasn't having another heart attack. I drove to the emergency department of the Grand Strand Medical Center for a consultation.

It wasn't long before Dr. Krates gave us the bad news; my tests showed three critical blockages in the veins leading to my heart. If he didn't operate on me, I would soon suffer a serious heart attack, and possibly die. Barb called our insurance company, and I was glad when they suggested I wait and have the surgery in Montreal. They recommended we fly, but I was pretty sure it wouldn't make that big of a difference if I drove.

Dr. Krates, however, didn't think I would last the time it would take to fly home, especially not without medical supervision. The insurance company finally agreed, and the surgery was set for the following morning.

It took roughly six hours for Dr. Krates to perform a triple bypass on me, after which I was put in the intensive care unit for two days. You can definitely see the difference from what Medicare gives you in Canada, versus insurance in the States. My room was like a hotel suite!

The evening before I was scheduled to be released, my heart stopped. All I can remember is hearing, "Code Blue", before I assume the doctors came and restarted my heart.

I woke up the following morning to a very terrified Barb, who was not pleased with me. As if it was my fault my heart stopped. Luckily, Linda had flown down to be with her.

. . .

IT TOOK two more days before I was discharged. Barb, Linda, and JP were all there to pick me up. I wasn't going to be able to drive back to Montreal, so Roger drove up with JP and Kay to drive the motorhome while JP and Linda took turns driving his car. I was incredibly touched by how they all dropped everything to be there for me and help me out.

ONLY SIX DAYS after undergoing major surgery, I was doing pretty well, even going on short walks. My family took this as an excellent sign, and decided we would go for supper at a restaurant in the mall. Their theory was that I had to eat anyway, so I might as well join them instead of eating alone in the motorhome. Believe me, this was not a good idea. I was exhausted just from sitting there, and practically had to be carried home. It was much too soon for me to venture out to restaurants.

JP AND LINDA drove home after the restaurant incident, but the rest of us stayed another week so the doctors could make sure I didn't have any complications from the surgery. I refused any future invites to go out, and spent the following days improving my condition before my next appointment. I was doing good, so Dr. Krates gave me the okay to go home.

Roger was the only one who could drive the motorhome, but we were all in a hurry to get back to Montreal, so he insisted on only stopping for fuel. We got there on October 1st.

It was another close call on my life. I think the stress from the government audit was the main cause, so I took it as a lesson to live each day as if it were my last, and to take every day one at a time.

38

"There is always a storm. There is always rain. Some experience it. Some live through it. And others are made from it."
- Shannon L. Alder

In January 1998, Quebec had its biggest ice storm in centuries, shutting down 80% of the main electrical grid and leaving most businesses and residences without power for twenty-two days. Montreal was declared a disaster area, with millions of people without heat, or power. In an essay once she was back in school, Chelsea called it, 'The Time Quebec Froze Over'. As it was, we were among the lucky ones, because I had equipped my home with three wood burning fireplaces, plus propane gas to heat our hot water tanks, and two generators to keep the kitchen and television running.

The fourteen of us – Barb and I, the kids, and grandkids – stayed in the house at the campground. I wasn't yet fully recovered from my triple bypass surgery, but together we were able to keep an eye on the campground, and keep the fireplaces running 24/7. We had more than enough wood, but it had to be brought into the garage to thaw out before we could use it. We went through roughly a cord of wood and forty litres of propane every day. Thanks to the campground, the fourteen of us lived pretty much the same as before the storm, although in closer quarters. We even let strangers use our commercial washrooms and showers, as so many people were without hot water.

Danny and Lynn lived close to a police station, so they were the first to get their power back. The past few weeks had been like a fun vacation for the kids, with movie rentals, new toys, and sleeping on the floor with their cousins like a sleepover party. Poor little Steve cried, "It's not fair. Why do we have to go home first?" when they left.

ONCE THE INITIAL fallout was over, we had to clean up the mess and repair all of the damage caused by the storm. Luckily, since we were in the disaster zone, we received government support to get up and running again. We were assigned eight employees from the unemployment roster - Danny and Sandra among them - for five weeks to remove all of the broken trees and branches. It was a giant task, but we were able to open in the spring, only slightly worse for the wear.

Me and Barbara at our fortieth anniversary party.

On April 10th 1998, Barb and I headed to Kenny Wong's to celebrate Amanda's 8th birthday. Boy, were we surprised when they brought us to a large room filled with all of our closest friends and family. Barb, who thought it was a surprise party for me, was shocked when she finally understood that it was for our 60th birthdays, and 40th wedding anniversary. Even Father Jerry, our local priest, was there so we could renew our vows. Then, after a delicious meal, we sang karaoke and danced the night away!

It was around this time that Lynn was diagnosed with breast cancer. She went through chemotherapy, as well as radiation therapy to make sure they removed it all. We hoped and prayed that she would make a full recovery, and thankfully, she went into remission. Barb and I got her a wig with real hair, so she could feel more like herself while she waited for hers to grow back.

As for my heart, it was doing better, and I was getting daily exercise, as well as weekly vita-flex massages from a professional, Bob Mariasine. He would bring his massage table and do it at the house, even convincing me to buy an inversion table of my own. I have to admit, I was open to anything that would keep me alive and healthy.

We made a lot of new purchases at the campground, and took advantage of the storm's damage to redo some of our original infrastructure, like our walk-in fridge, counters, shelves, windows, and roof. We had to replace many hydro poles and electrical lines.

I also commissioned a beautiful conference table from a famed Belgian woodworker in the neighborhood. I made it round, like King Arthur's Round Table, with enough room for twelve to sit comfortably.

39

"One cannot think well, love well, sleep well, if one has not dined well."
-Virginia Woolf

I had big plans for the campground in 1999, notably replacing the public washroom facilities in our wooded area, as well as our 'E' section. The renovations were necessary to maintain our five-star rating. We were one of only eight to receive top marks, out of the 780 campgrounds registered in Quebec. Our planned expenditures for the year always took into account what would maintain our rating, what would bring in more revenues, and what would make our customers happy.

I GOT into full renovation mode, working on the washrooms in our main building to start. I still needed to work out the architectural, mechanical and electrical plans for the new washroom facilities, so I figured it would be nice to do them in Florida. I had just purchased a 38-foot motorhome, a Monaco Diplomat, so Barb and I took it for a test drive!

We returned to the cold of Montreal and got straight to work rearranging the shelves in our convenience store and building the new washroom facilities. In order to maintain our five-star rating, we needed to have a certain number of washrooms and showers per so many sites, but I also wanted them to be modern; something you would expect to find in a hotel rather than the middle of the woods.

We only had a couple of months to complete the projects before the season came into full swing. All the demolition and construction was carried out by my staff, with the exception of the bricklaying on the exteriors, which I contracted to Yvon Lapolice, one of our campers. He did the work with Marco, who you might remember as the little boy who used to follow me around when I first purchased shares in the campground.

We finished the projects in May, just before the campground got busy.

ROBERT WYNGAERT

Me and Barbara at Le Continental.

That summer, we discovered what would become our favorite restaurant, Le Continental, in Quebec City. Their cuisine is Franco-Italian, but the major selling point is their flambé dishes, and the Caesar salads they make right at your table. After the meal, no matter how full you are from all the delicious courses that came before, you have to find room for their Brazilian Coffees and Crêpes Suzette! We brought most of our friends and family there over the years, and recommended it to every single camper who was headed for Quebec City.

Barbara and I in Shediac.

WE ALSO SPENT two weeks exploring the East Coast, mostly with Roger and Kay. We visited New Brunswick, Prince Edward Island, and Nova Scotia. It was another wonderful vacation for the books, and I can say with certainty that I never ate so much lobster in my entire life!

40

Camping Alouette Inc. is a respected, successful Company. We want to make it better for our customers, our employees and for the community in which we work. Our goal is to be the recognized leaders in the campground industry.

-Camping Alouette Mission Statement

BY 2000, we had increased our yearly profit reinvestment from roughly $100 000 to more like $250 000. This was mostly because the campground was bringing in more of a profit, but we were also building a reputation, and we wanted to keep it up. We were top-rated not only in Quebec, but with all of the American camping associations: Good Sam's Club, Woodalls, AAA, etc. We made it a part of our Mission Statement to be recognized as leaders in the camping industry.

In light of this, we focused on 'revamping' everything, to make our roads, landscaping and signage fit better with our five-star branding. There was a house in Beloeil where the trees were all shaped as different things, so we asked the owner, Guy Bernard, to come and do something with our hedges. He turned them into trains, deer, an owl, a squirrel, and Big Ben, with new additions as the years went on!

Linda, me, Rene Raiche, Lynn, Sandra, and Barbara at Camping Quebec.

That fall at the Camping Quebec convention, we won the award for best customer service! I made it a point when training my staff to always greet the customers with 'Hello, how can I help you?", and Sandra continued the tradition, urging the employees to greet every customer like they were valued and important, no matter how busy we were.

I don't know if this had anything to do with the award, but we had recently begun hiring our grandchildren to work at the campground. I started them out with the same salary I'd given my children back when they started working, which wasn't much. However, I kept a close eye on them, and gave them raises as they were able to take on more responsibilities. It was important for me to be able to provide this opportunity for them, to never have to look for a job, and to have a stable start in life. I didn't want them to have to worry about things like being laid off the night before their wedding, or having to decide between a transfer to a different province, and being without a job.

Even more important was that they learn a good work ethic and the proper skills, so whichever job they chose in the future would be open to them. They worked hard, long hours, with a smile, and made me proud every single day. By the end of their first summers, they were making more in a couple of hours than I had in a week at Daniel Kiely's!

AT THE END of the year, in addition to my usual planning for campground expenditures, I made Barbara a proposal for future vacations. I had big plans for weekend trips closer to home, longer road trips in Canada and the States, as well as flights to Europe and the Caribbean. After most of my life spent making plans to build up my career and wealth, I was now making plans to live my life and enjoy it. Obviously, I wanted to ensure that we could maintain our way of life, but never at the expense of the things that made it worth living. My main priorities were now to make our campground the best in Canada, but more importantly, to support and guide our children and grandchildren, so they could succeed as well.

41

"Whether you think you can or you think you can't, you're right."
-Henry Ford

In January 2002, I went through a phase where I had absolutely no motivation. I had many ideas and dreams I wanted to accomplish, but I could not find the energy to plan them out and implement them. I sat down and thought of things I could do in the short term, as well as long term, to bring back my drive and ambition. Part of my attitude was possibly based on the fact that I kept trying to get the permits to build a recreation hall at the campground, but kept getting refused by the city.

Well, after making my list, I decided that instead of continuing to try and get their permission, I would start building now and ask for forgiveness later. I did not want to give them the opportunity to tell me my rec hall was a safety hazard that had to come down, so I built it going above and beyond all the safety rules and building codes. I used commercial trusses, made everything thicker than it needed to be, and even surrounded the interior of the building with a shoulder-level brick wall to prevent any fires. It was as sturdy as rec halls come, and attached to a state-of-the-art RV Wash. I had used many of them during my travels, but our Canadian climate gave an open-air

RV wash a limited time of operation every year. So, we made ours fully-enclosed; the first of its kind in all of North America, as far as I know.

Our recreation hall and RV Wash.

Obviously, the city wasn't happy. Contractors were told they couldn't work on the project, since we didn't have a permit, so I had to rely on my own employees, and close friends.

Eventually, my case was brought in front of a judge. I knew I would be in trouble, but I prayed they wouldn't make me tear it down.

Luckily, the judge took our side, apparently wondering why every other campground was allowed to build a rec hall, yet they kept refusing me. I knew that the city wanted to get rid of us so they could build houses and make a lot more in taxes, but I obviously couldn't use that in my defense.

I wasn't there for the trial, but I found out the outcome when the mayor of St-Mathieu-de-Beloeil called and told me to come and get my permit. It sounded like the words were physically painful for him to say. I knew I would have to pay for it in the future, but for now I had my hall and my RV wash. I was happy!

. . .

We put the hall to good use, starting that May, when we hosted a Country Western Festival. It was supposed to be an opportunity to bring in more revenue, but we ultimately found it to be a lot more trouble than it was worth for the business. However, from a personal standpoint, the Wyngaerts had a great time, as it reignited our love of country music. We quickly found a teacher and started Line Dancing Lessons. Our hall was the site of many weddings, birthday parties, anniversary parties...the girls were excellent at decorating for all of my events, but Lynn really went above and beyond to make any party extra special. Her Halloween parties were legendary, with ghosts, skeletons, and even tombstones!

In October, we went to the Camping Quebec convention, pretty confident that we would be coming home with the Award for Innovation we submitted for. I couldn't imagine what any other campground could have done to compete with our fully equipped recreation hall and never-before-seen RV Wash. We were also the first in Canada to have wireless internet on most of our sites, thanks to JP.

I was flabbergasted when someone else went up to claim our prize. I looked to Sandra and Linda, to make sure I heard right. They shrugged, as if to say 'we tried our best', but they were also crushed. I can't even remember what the winner's innovation had been.

It wasn't until the end of the night, when they announced the Campground of the Year, that they shocked me by calling, "Camping Alouette!"

Apparently, they read the proposal Sandra submitted for the Innovation Award and decided we deserved better. I was overwhelmed by happiness and pride for everything we had achieved since purchasing a run-down plot of land. I had a passion to be the best in what we do and to meet all of my objectives. I wanted to maintain my basic principles of loyalty and honesty.

Barbara and I at Camping Quebec.

Barbara with our Dynasty motorhome.

At the end of the season, Barb and I purchased a 2002 Monaco Dynasty, our biggest and most expensive motorhome. It was 42-feet, fully equipped, and cost more than most houses. However, it was on my bucket list, and even Barb was thrilled with the Whirlpool bath she got to relax in, and the washer/dryer combo. It also gave us an excuse to plan another family trip to Walt Disney World, all fourteen of us.

Barbara, Linda, Sandra, me, Eric, Amanda, Rikki, Chelsea, Lynn, and Steve at Disney in 2002.

Things were going well for us financially, so once we got home from Disney, I focused on what I believed would be my legacy; the Wyngaert Estates. I purchased land on one of our hills, bordering the golf course, and made plans to build a gated community where my family would live; Barb and I, the kids, and someday the grandkids. I designed a block plan to present to the city for approval, along with details, and a schedule. I was so encouraged when they told me it looked like a good plan and should be approved at their next meeting. I began to clear the land, to provide space for the houses. I planned to have nine lots of an acre each.

42

"Two of the greatest gifts we can give our children are roots and wings."
-Hodding Carter

The Summer of 2003 brought a lot of changes to the campground, some visible and others not. Our internet was very slow, relying on antennas and modems that we rented out to campers. You would think they were coming camping to escape from work and enjoy nature, but our clientele was the kind that appreciated us cutting down trees so they could get a better wi-fi signal. Which we did, removing a grassy wooded area to make 'wooded' RV sites in its place, for those who wanted to feel like they were camping, while enjoying modern amenities.

As far as the internet, JP and Paul installed fiber optics so the entire park had reliable wireless internet. It was quite the investment, but worth it for our campers.

AT THE END of the season, instead of going on a road trip, Barb and I took a flight to Europe.

Paris was different from any other place we'd experienced before. It seemed like everyone there was slim, smoked, and carried a cell phone. I'd had a phone in my car, back when I was working at Pratt, and thought I was pretty cool at the time, but I couldn't imagine wanting to allow myself to be reached 24/7, no matter where I went.

I loved the architecture, and how 'old' in Paris meant thousands of years, rather than the hundreds of years when referring to Quebec buildings. Even how the buildings are narrow in the front, then expand out to fit the streets. Barb enjoyed how fancy everyone dressed.

We spent a day exploring the Louvre, but I easily could have spent three. It was so interesting to see the artifacts of how people lived in the past.

We were both shocked to see how many animals were allowed in restaurants, and how we had to pay to use the washrooms, which were subpar compared to ours, sometimes consisting of nothing more than a hole in the ground.

We left Paris to visit Belgium; the land of my ancestors. We visited the Manneken

Pis statue and purchased a few small brass replicas for souvenirs.

The evening we were scheduled to return to Paris, there was an incident that delayed the train. By the time we got to Paris, it was early morning, so the metro wasn't running yet. I tried to find us a taxi as we walked towards our hotel, which was roughly six kilometers away. We didn't get far before running into a police road block.

It wasn't until the officer approached us, hand on her gun, asking what we were doing in such a dangerous area, that we found out it wasn't safe.

I explained to her about the trip to Belgium and the train delay in French, but my Quebec accent was very different from her Parisian one. She asked where we were from, correctly pegging us as lost tourists. I told her we were from Quebec, and it was our first time in Europe, so she offered to take us to our hotel in their Paddy wagon, as they were taking down the road block.

It was quite the experience!

The officers all asked about things in Quebec, insisting that they would love to visit our country. I told them to look us up if they ever did!

With the Manneken Pis Statue in Belgium.

43

"Dance like nobody's watching; love like you've never been hurt. Sing like nobody's listening; live like it's heaven on earth."
-Mark Twain

Amanda, Rikki, me, Paul, and Linda in Punta Cana, 2004.

We took a family vacation to Breezes Punta Cana in February 2004. It was truly paradise, to be in the sun with my family, drinking all the fancy drinks and enjoying delicious meals without having to pay anything extra. We were such a large group, with beautiful young girls, so all of the animators knew us, and often sat to eat their meals with us. I participated in more activities than I ever had before, with dancing lessons, Beach Olympics, Water Aerobics, Water Polo...you name it, we tried it.

It was during the second week that we told one of the animators about Chelsea being a dancer, taking ballet, tap, and jazz since she was a toddler. We thought it was just fake enthusiasm when he asked her a bunch of questions, until he invited her to dance in one of their shows later on in the week. I think Chelsea wanted to relax and not make such a big deal of it, but we quickly convinced her to say yes. She rehearsed for a couple of days with the dancers, then blew us all away as a pink spotted white cat in their production of Cats. I had been watching her dance shows for years, and knew she was talented, but I was amazed at how it took her less than two days to look like she had been dancing with them for years. I was so proud, telling everyone who would listen that she was my granddaughter.

ONCE I GOT BACK to work at the campground, I had plans to build a large garage, where we would be able to repair our equipment, and store it in the winter. Unfortunately, we were having problems with the city, so I let it go and extended a plateau area to the storage instead. We didn't need to fence it in, as it was so far removed from circulation, and we even kept it graveled. We charged the same price whether it was asphalted or not, so it didn't make sense to spend the money on asphalt when the demand was there either way.

SANDRA'S FAMILY was going to renovate their house, but when the architect told them it would be smarter to move, they decided to build their house on the Wyngaert Estate instead. They moved in with us at the beginning of the summer, while we started work on a fancy, cement house for them. Sandra designed it to be the house of their dreams, with grand staircases, walk-in closets, reading nooks, a wine cellar, an in-law suite...it truly was a mansion.

AS FAR AS the summer went, we hardly noticed a difference, as they were usually there every day for work anyway. There was a motorhome in our storage that went into foreclosure, so we accepted the unit to make up for the unpaid storage fees. Once it was sanitized, JP and Sandra moved into it while Amanda took the spare bedroom and Paul slept in the basement. Amanda listened to me as I sang to her and told stories of my youth in the mornings.

In November, I was invited to a special evening for the Richelieu Valley Chamber of

Commerce, and was honoured to receive their 'Grand Richelois 2004-2005 Award' for my contributions to the local economy.

Family vacations had become our yearly tradition, so we went to Mexico, at the Occidental Grand Flamenco Xcaret, for the Christmas holidays in 2004-2005.

Our resort was situated next to Xcaret, a cultural park which I would compare to a Mexican Disney. I think they called it an amusement park, but it was also a nature reserve, with wild animals both on land and in the ocean. There were recreations of traditional villages, and I was mesmerized by the 'Ha: Breath of Life' show we got to see in the evening. I was expecting fire dancing, like we saw in Hawai'i, but I was not expecting a game of field hockey where the puck was on fire. Or for all of the statues that surrounded us to come to life and participate in the show. It was absolutely magical!

We spent another day snorkelling in underwater caves, which was more incredible than I could have imagined. I had been snorkelling before, but nothing compared to the snorkelling we did on this trip. One moment we were in complete darkness, and the next we were bathed in light from a tiny opening in the ceiling, sometimes having to swim through tunnels to get to the next section.

UNBELIEVABLE BUT TRUE

Barbara, Chelsea, Eric, Rikki, Steve, JP, Sandra, Paul, Amanda, Linda, Cazzie, Lynn, and I in Mexico, 2005.

44

"You can have it all. You just can't have it all at once."
-Oprah Winfrey

In 2005, we decided we preferred flying to hotels with the family rather than driving alone in the motorhome, so we sold it. We only received half of what we paid for it, making it a terrible investment financially. Cars and motorhomes usually are, but the memories we made traveling over the past two decades were worth it.

After hearing all of our stories, Ronnie and Anne were also looking to try an all-inclusive vacation, so we thought it would be fun to go the four of us together. When we saw the Sandals Royal Bahamian resort was 65% off, we immediately booked for April 2nd.

The service was above and beyond our wildest dreams, even without tipping, which is forbidden there. It was only for a week, but Sandals became the standard through which we measured all subsequent vacations. For the next fifteen years, we went over eighteen times to Sandals resorts, even earning a free week through their Sandals Select program.

Ronnie, Anne, me, and Barbara in Bahamas.

Back at the campground, we were working hard, building Sandra's house. We were still going off of a verbal permit, but it hadn't caused any problems yet. When Hydro Quebec told us they couldn't put in the electricity without an address, we directed them to the city, who gave us 3451 de l'industrie.

The house was taking shape, so you

could walk the halls and recognize all of the different rooms. The windows had arrived, and the entire structure was built by the time the city advised us to stop any further work on the house.

We were incredibly confused, but apparently, our permit had been denied. After a verbal approval, months of construction, and hundreds of thousands of dollars, they were going back on their word.

There had to be a misunderstanding, so we went to the mayor, who told us we could get our permit as long as we closed the campground. They saw it as a win-win situation. With the campground gone, they could build a housing development, which we'd already started.

I was so discouraged. We had built the campground from the ground up over the past three decades, and now they were making me decide between my family business and the family legacy I wanted to build upon it. Unfortunately, the Wyngaert Estates were intrinsically tied to Camping Alouette, and I did not want to have anything to do with this manipulative and treacherous municipality. We abandoned Sandra's dream house and started listening to the offers people made to buy the campground.

UNFORTUNATELY, Roger was diagnosed with Alzheimer's Disease around this time. We had noticed small things at first, like when he got lost going to places we knew well, or needed my help to install his satellite. You see, Roger was incredibly gifted at repairing any kind of motor or appliance. It was like he just looked at them and immediately knew how they worked. Which was why it was so heartbreaking when he came to the campground to repair one of our dryers, took it all apart, then couldn't figure out how to put it back together.

45

"Letting go doesn't mean giving up, it means moving on."
-Unknown

In February 2006, we met with professionals to prepare the documentation necessary for the eventual sale of the campground. It was very hectic, as we had offers coming in one after the other. We'd had offers ever since we built up the campground's reputation, but had never entertained them like we were now. It took time to analyze each one.

Fay, Barbara, Kay, Anne, Roger, me, and Ronnie in Atlantic City.

In July, Barb and I went to Atlantic City, forty-eight years after we first went for our honeymoon. This time, we stayed at the Tahj-Mahal Hotel, and could afford to go into any shop or casino we wanted. We even got to participate in a version of 'The Price is Right'!

When we got back from the trip, I was shocked to see that my weight had reached 240 lbs. I decided to do something about it, hiring a nutritionist to meet with me on a weekly basis, and eventually got back down to 199lbs by the end of the year.

In October, I refused a large offer from Parkbridge, a company that owned many RV communities throughout Canada. We liked the idea that Parkbridge would keep it as a campground, and that they had so much experience in the broader camping industry. We even liked Dave Rozycki, one of the owners we met with, but we felt our campground was worth a lot more than they offered.

46

"Don't cry because it's over, smile because it happened."
-Dr. Seuss

I loved treating my family to experiences I knew they would enjoy, but wouldn't purchase for themselves. Barb and I spent many a weekend dining at the Continental, or the Baccara in Gatineau, bringing those closest to us, giving them an evening they wouldn't soon forget.

In the Spring of 2007, I brought the entire family to Quebec City so they could experience Le Continental, many of them for the first time. I was so excited to share Caesar salad made from scratch at your table, flambé meals and desserts, as well as five-star service with all of them. One of my favorite parts of the Continental, other than being treated like a beloved regular, is spending hours eating delicious food with the people I love.

IN EARLY 2007, Lynn's cancer came back. In another example of the medical system failing, every time she went in and described her pain, sharing her fears that it was cancer, they told her it was a herniated disk, or something equally innocuous. Losing weight and getting massages were their recommended treatments, until they saw the spots on her lungs and realized they'd been wrong.

On May 6TH, Lynn was admitted to the hospital. They'd been administering chemotherapy treatments, but things were not improving. At first, she was in good spirits, figuring out how to watch her tv shows on a computer (before Netflix went digital), but we could see that she was not doing well. The cancer was in her lungs and her bones, making it hard for her to breathe, and she was in constant pain. After a few weeks, she asked if she could go home to be more comfortable, so we made sure she had everything she needed to make that happen.

. . .

ROBERT WYNGAERT

IN THE MIDDLE of the night between May 30th and 31st, we got a call from my son Danny saying Lynn took a turn for the worse, so an ambulance was bringing them to the hospital. We rushed there to meet them, while Sandra and Linda went to his house to look after the boys, who were still sleeping.

Ethel and Mike, Lynn's parents, joined us at the hospital, so we were there when she took her last breath.

WHEN WE TOLD Steve and Eric, they decided that they still wanted to go to school, so the other grandchildren went as well. Danny and Linda went to make the funeral arrangements, while the rest of us sought the comfort of each other at the campground.

By lunchtime, all of the grandkids were there with us as we tried to process what had happened. Lynn wasn't the first person I loved who died, but she wasn't like my parents and Barb's, she was like my child. Only forty-four years old, with two children still in high school. It wasn't right, and it didn't make sense.

OVER THE NEXT FEW DAYS, we planned her funeral, making program booklets, folding pink breast cancer ribbons, bringing the boys to buy suits...it was a period of intense darkness. We tried our best to put on a brave face for the boys, encouraging them to go to the movies with their cousins, but nobody was even remotely okay.

We had to cancel the first aid course we were supposed to have that weekend, and closed the entire campground on June 4th, the day of the funeral. We still had campers, but every store employee, every grounds worker, every longtime camper…everyone was at the church. We had a group, West Coast Connections, that came every year, and completely forgot to warn them or have them pay their bill…we just shut down.

The funeral was held at the Our Lady of Fatima Church, where most of the family went every Sunday. There were so many people there that they didn't even fit inside the church. Every seat was taken, people were standing in the back, and once the service was over, we saw that there were people waiting outside and in the hallways. Lynn was loved!

Losing her changed everything in our family. For years, we had developed a flow at the campground, with Sandra tackling days, Lynn working nights, and Danny handling the grounds. In one fell swoop, we lost Lynn, Danny went into a depression, and it took a very long time for any of us to feel okay again. It didn't help that for years, campers would come in and ask us, "Where is Lynn?" or the office staff would pull out a storage contract and start crying when they recognized her handwriting, while the client looked on in confusion. The frustration that had pushed me to sell the campground before was nothing compared to the grief that showed us we couldn't go on like this anymore.

WE HAD A STRING OF OFFERS, and people who came close to buying the campground, but they all ultimately fell through. After a few more close calls, we got into negotiations with Parkbridge, who were still very interested.

. . .

Even with the possibility of an impending sale, we treated the campground like it would stay in our family for generations. In July, we drew up plans to hook up to the newly installed municipal sewer system, which we had been fighting to have for the last twenty-five years. We used one of our campers, Roger Gauthier, as our excavation contractor, because I like supporting the people who support us. Plus, we knew he had a vested interest in the project. He estimated it would cost $140 000, which was steep for something none of the campers would necessarily notice, but it was a lot cheaper than the alternative.

Years before, there was an issue with the septic system at Camping Lac du Repos, so the owner went into the septic tank to fix it on his own. His son-in-law was waiting outside, so when the owner stopped responding, his son-in-law went in after him. Within minutes, the two of them, as well as a camper who tried to help, all died from the toxic fumes inside. After watching the pain and sorrow that family went through because of their septic system, any amount of money to get hooked up to the municipal sewer system was worth it.

Parkbridge Lifestyle Communities finally came to their senses and realized they did not want to miss out on the opportunity of a lifetime with Camping Alouette. They presented us with a new offer, which was more reasonable, but still less than I believed the campground was worth.

We analyzed it, then made a list of all of the campground's assets to show them how much more they were getting than what meets the eye. Sandra typed it all up for me, using the MasterCard commercial format. After listing all of the assets and their worth, she wrote, "Our five-star reputation: Priceless." She also included, "Add a million to your offer, and consider it our counter-offer" more to be funny than because we meant it, as we were sure nobody would settle for a million dollars over their offer price.

We were absolutely shocked when they accepted.

Suddenly, the campground was sold, but we hadn't really intended to accept it. I talked it over with my family, as well as trusted professionals, and we decided it was in our best interest to go through with it. Not because we'd inadvertently agreed to it, but because I was tired of the physical labor and mental stress the campground involved, and none of my grandchildren planned to take it over.

We didn't believe the sale was real until the papers were signed, as we had gone through many offers and verbal agreements that fell through, often at a heavy cost to us.

ON NOVEMBER 15TH, we met at our lawyer's office and signed the papers, making it official. I sold Camping Alouette, the business I operated for over thirty years with the help of my family. After signing, our lawyer hinted that it was customary for the buyers to take the old owners out for a fancy meal to celebrate, so we went to Vargas for a very long lunch.

IN THE FOLLOWING WEEKS, I felt so many mixed emotions. The campground was not only a place where we all came to work, it was also the place where we enjoyed countless parties with family and friends...it was home. Because of this, and the fact that we didn't want to have to go

ROBERT WYNGAERT

through the trouble of moving, we negotiated with Parkbridge so we could live in the house for the rest of our lives, rent-free.

Camping Alouette in the Eighties.

UNBELIEVABLE BUT TRUE

Camping Alouette when we sold it.

EPILOGUE

Barb and I were never going to be able to enjoy our retirement while still living at the campground, where customers frequently interrupted our dinners and evenings with requests for propane or campsites, so my niece, Johanne Wyngaert, helped us purchase a new home. With a million dollar view of Mont-Saint-Hilaire, and the beautiful Richelieu River flowing below, it truly was like a dream come true.

It was hard at first, adjusting to a life of retirement, so I would go consult at the campground and Barb would stop by with meals for the employees. As time went on, I put that time and energy into our new home, turning it into a summer paradise with beautiful flowers, a pool, a fireplace, a party boat...everything you could wish for. I started playing golf to stay active in the summer, and the kids even bought us a Wii for Christmas. We thought it was a silly gift, but now we play it almost every day, and Barb can beat anyone at the age assessment game. We didn't have to escape our busy lives anymore, so we had people over for any and all occasions, both happy and sad; friends, family, and strangers. We traveled to all kinds of all-inclusive resorts with groups ranging from just Barb and I, to over 35 people! We had health scares, hospital visits, and surgeries - way more than any of us wanted. But we are still here, and doing better than ever. As the

Miranda Esmonde-White book recommends, I am aging backwards!

The best part is that I got to be there for my children and grandchildren like I never had before. I got to know my children through boat rides, weekend trips, and vacations better than I had when they were living with me, and I was privileged to become their friend.

We got to watch as our grandchildren went farther than I could have imagined with their educations, earning MBAs and doctorates, working and studying across the globe, from London to New Zealand. Some of them are even starting their own families! I am so incredibly proud of everything they have accomplished so far, and I know this is just the beginning of all the wonderful things they will do.

I believe my greatest accomplishment is my family, without whom none of my successes would have been possible. That is why I cannot express the joy and emotions I felt holding my great-grandsons, Harry and Nathan, for the first time. While writing my autobiography, I realized that in working so hard to ensure that my family was provided for, I often missed out on precious moments with them. Decades went by where I spent 99% of my time working multiple jobs, but very little of it with my wife and children. I was blessed to have the campground, where we all worked so close together, but I vowed not to repeat the same mistakes with this new generation. Watching them grow up gives Barb and I another reason to live longer. I have no pictures of myself with my grandfather, but Nathan and Harry will have many. They are, after all, my legacy.

May God Bless You and Guide You.

Bob

WYNGAERT WEALTH ESSENTIALS

I had never expected us to sell the campground in my lifetime, but I was glad that thanks to Linda, we had effective tax planning in place, and our finances were taken care of. I invested the proceeds of the sale in a diversified portfolio under Linda's management. She put a plan in place to pay me dividends to replace the income we had been receiving from the campground.

If you remember what happened in September 2008, you know that November 2007 was not the best time to have invested my life savings in the stock market. Thank God I took some money out to purchase my dream home before the markets crashed. I did not need to finance the house, but I made sure I had access to a line of credit, just in case.

That line of credit came in handy a few months later, with the value of my portfolio falling every day and nothing but bad news on the economy. Linda suggested that I use my line of credit for cash flow, to stop the bleeding until the markets rebounded.

In the meantime, she sold my investments and bought similar ones the same day to crystallize the capital losses. I was able to carry these losses back against the gains that I had on the sale of the business the previous year which resulted in a sizeable tax refund. It was a scary and unpredictable time, but in the long term everything worked out. I am so happy that I had Linda's guidance and expertise during this tough time. She made the best of what could have been a nightmare!

There is no better financial team out there, as far as I'm concerned. Linda, Steve, and Sandra offer over twenty years of experience, knowledge, and the human touch that puts them above all the rest. You will not regret your decision to invest with Wyngaert Wealth Essentials.

AMANDA LYNN PETRIN

My granddaughter, who helped me with this book, has published four novels of her own. Shards of Glass is a Contemporary Young Adult novel, while **The Owens Chronicles** is an Urban Fantasy trilogy consisting of Prophecy, Destiny, and Legacy. They are available in ebook, paperback, and hardcover, wherever books are sold.

You can find her at
www.amandalynnpetrin.com

JOHANNE WYNGAERT

If you are looking to sell or purchase a home in the Montreal Area, my niece is the best in the business and goes above and beyond for her clients.

ACKNOWLEDGMENTS

This book involved the help of my family to make it possible, and fill in the blanks when my memory failed me. I am enormously grateful.

A special thanks to Amanda, who truly made this book happen, and to Sandra, for her invaluable editorial insights. I also appreciate the feedback and proofreading I received from Linda, Chelsea, Rikki, Paul, and Samantha. They all took time out of their busy schedules to make this book the best it could be.

And finally, I want to thank my wife for putting up with me during our sixty-five years together, making all of my dreams and wishes come true.

ABOUT THE AUTHOR

Robert Wyngaert has been a gentleman bouncer, supervised the weekend shifts at Canada Packers, owned a restaurant, worked his way up the corporate ladder at Pratt & Whitney, and built a five-star campground from the ground up, but his greatest accomplishment is his family.

He lives in Quebec with his beautiful wife, Barbara. Whenever there isn't a global pandemic, you will find their children and grandchildren there every week for Sunday night dinner.

www.ingramcontent.com/pod-product-compliance
Lightning Source LLC
Chambersburg PA
CBHW021422070526
44577CB00001B/15